TUSCAN
& ANDALUSIAN REFLECTIONS

TUSCAN
& ANDALUSIAN REFLECTIONS

20 Beautiful Homes Inspired By Old World Architecture

BASSENIAN / LAGONI ARCHITECTS

A Book By Bassenian/Lagoni Architects
Copyright © 2005 by Bassenian/Lagoni Architects (hardcover)
Copyright © 2008 by Bassenian/Lagoni Architects (softcover)

Library of Congress Control Number:
2004095720

International Standard Book Number:
ISBN-13: 978-0-9721539-2-8 (hardcover)
ISBN-10: 0-9721539-2-6 (hardcover)
ISBN-13: 978-0-9721539-5-9 (softcover)
ISBN-10: 0-9721539-5-0 (softcover)

Published by Bassenian/Lagoni Architects
2031 Orchard Drive, Suite 100
Newport Beach, CA 92660-0753
Phone: 949-553-9100
Fax: 949-553-0548
www.bassenianlagoni.com

Corporate
Chairman & CEO: Aram Bassenian, AIA
President: Carl Lagoni, AIA
Executive Vice President: Lee Rogaliner
Senior Principals: Scott Adams, AICP
                  David Kosco, AIA
                  Jeffrey LaFetra, AIA
Principals: Steven Dewan, AIA
            Kevin Karami
            Jeff Lake, AIA
            Ken Niemerski, AIA

Book Production
Editorial Director: Aram Bassenian, AIA
Editor-in-Chief: Rickard Bailey, Bailey Consulting, Inc.
Writer: Laura Hurst Brown, Brownhurst Enterprises
Design/Art Director: Edie Motoyama
Art Director/Designer, Cover Design: Zareh Marzbetuny, ZM Design
Floor Plan Graphics: Jennifer Cram, Edie Motoyama
Editorial Coordinator: Debby Owens
Assistant to the Editorial Director: Kele Dooley

Prepress by Toppan Hong Kong

Printed in Hong Kong by Toppan Printing

10   9   8   7   6   5   4   3   2   1

Contents

Acknowledgements

by Aram Bassenian, AIA

This book represents a selection of recent designs by an architectural practice that spans over three decades. Such longevity is only possible due to the contribution of many dedicated people. So we must begin by acknowledging the talents of the Bassenian/Lagoni team of architects, planners, colorists, graphic artists and administrators. This group of one hundred has consistently exhibited an unabashed passion towards housing and has worked with total commitment toward the advancement of residential architecture.

A major debt of gratitude goes to the builders whose special projects appear between these covers. This is a new generation of experienced entrepreneurs who take responsibility for the creation of exemplary communities. The unique homes and projects displayed on these pages show an effort that goes beyond financial gain. They give birth to a vision, they select and lead a design team to its translation, and finally they execute the vision to perfection. The result is the creation of superb communities and lasting contributions to the built environment. This is how the art of homebuilding continues to improve.

We are also extremely fortunate to have the support of so many allied professionals in our field. We are fully aware that without interior designers, landscape architects and structural engineers—to name a few—our homes would not achieve this heightened level of presentation. The annotated project list gives appropriate credit to those fine firms whose excellent work appears throughout this book. And, to be sure, no presentation of work at this caliber would have been possible without the collaboration of extremely talented photographers. We, the architects who practice in the arena of production housing, are privileged to see our design reach a satisfying level of completion as "models" are prepared for public viewing. We are doubly fortunate when these examples are professionally photographed by a cadre of competent and experienced craftsmen in our homebuilding trade. Their artistry gives life to our work and delight to our eyes at every viewing. We thank those photographers warmly, and we happily credit them on the opening pages of each project.

We also dedicate this book to that long list of individuals in our industry without whose long-term friendship and good will our firm would not have evolved and prospered. It has taken many years to build a strong organization internally—but this has not been accomplished without the support, encouragement and recognition of a host of external industry executives, staff and professionals. It has been the continuity of work provided by a national homebuilding industry that has enabled us to attract and sustain the talented people with whom we have grown and evolved over these past thirty years.

And regarding the specifics of this book, we express deep appreciation to Edie Motoyama and Zareh Marzbetuny for their exquisite book design. And our thanks to Jennifer Cram for creating the handsome floor plan graphics and Laura Hurst Brown for her insightful observations in expressive and beautifully descriptive words.

Lastly, even before the publication of our first volume, *Pure California*, we were privileged to meet a very experienced publishing professional who signed on as our Editor-in-Chief. It has been with the assistance and conviction of Rickard Bailey that a select part of our work and accompanying imagery has been cataloged and bound, and has taken its place among the shelves next to a long list of American residential architectural books. His guidance in the step-by-step production of each volume has been invaluable.

Foreword

Architecture In Harmony With A New Era

by A. David Kovach

It was the very early 1990s. The Irvine Company, landowner and world-renowned master planner of 100,000 acres in the virtual center of Orange County, was undertaking in earnest the planning of its most prized parcel—the last major undeveloped 2,500 acres of oceanfront property in Southern California, a place today known as Newport Coast. We had asked several noteworthy design firms to bring their preliminary ideas addressing the "hilltown" concept envisioned by company chairman Donald Bren.

Aram Bassenian came to that meeting with a unique study of insightful images and took us on a tour of the details important to creation of the hilltown experience. It soon became apparent that this was something he had studied— something he had lived. The images were pure, authentic, inspiring. History will likely show the early 1990s as the beginning point for a whole new era in the marketplace: an environment fundamentally different from anything we understood previously. To know we are in this new period is to look back on the previous formative century and be aware that it opened with the systemic thought of Henry Ford and closed with the expansive thought of Bill Gates. The new century dawned with a heightened appreciation that superior performance in the marketplace is quite simply a function of superior thought applied in just the right way.

Several important influences are converging to contribute to today's newly defined marketplace. After more than 60 years of prolific production, we find ourselves quite well-housed, especially in the best locations. Optimal market performance is based ever less on "demand" than "discretion." Burgeoning digital technology appears to be bringing with it as much speed and intensity as it once promised to ease. It has been theorized that much of the recent emergence of "retro" or historic-based design expression (seen mostly in cars and houses) is providing a kind of psychic-comfort "base" to balance one's life being otherwise driven at an ever-increasing pace by new technology.

In short, there is growing conflict between previous production formulas and technological innovations. At the center of this conflict, a new force is being exerted: the empowered, complicated, discretionary customer. In new housing, there is a place where the stricture of the builder and the emotion of the customer are resolved. Traditionally, that place was dominated by the builder perspective. Today, the more enlightened builder willingly gives substantially more weight and consideration to the customer. In this process, the architect is charged with finding and balancing such a place with design.

For nearly 35 years, Aram Bassenian and Carl Lagoni have brought their considerable talents to that very important place and witnessed their work expand globally. The pages of this volume are filled with illustrations of superior thought well applied. To a more insightful, discretionary customer, increasing customization is thoughtfully finessed. Fully integrated designs, inspired by authentic historic forms, portray substantive, *real*-feeling homes. Total compositions emphasize the home as retreat and sanctuary, and the careful orchestration of a myriad of details conveys simple elegance.

The designs displayed in this work were inspired by, and specifically do not attempt replication of, their European antecedents. As such, they are appropriately termed Tuscan and Andalusian "reflections." Properly, the homes speak to a quality referencing their specific environments, both physical and market. As always, the successful experience of these homes in the marketplace tells us about where we have been, where we are today, and where we are headed. These plans physically symbolize the sum of the unique thoughts and processes of the Bassenian/Lagoni brand.

Superior market performance in our new era results from the collaboration of intimate market knowledge informing inspired design. The insight and artistry that Aram shared with us at the Irvine Company in the early 1990s were in harmony with the evolving marketplace and continue to flourish today. Going forward, we eagerly anticipate where Bassenian/Lagoni creativity will take us in the future.

Introduction

by Aram Bassenian, AIA & Carl Lagoni, AIA

For over three decades, Bassenian/Lagoni Architects has concentrated on the design of residential communities. We take pride in the knowledge that our craft has touched the lives of hundreds of thousands of families across California and the United States. This book represents a slice from our recent work, which—by our measure—has been elevated by the concurrence of an extraordinary surge in the homebuilding industry and the vision of sophisticated and highly experienced builder clients.

It's a carefully constructed collection representing new architectural ground and, before you begin your armchair tour of these upscale Tuscan- and Andalusian-inspired homes, we would like to offer some suggestions on how to view them. Allow us to guide you through these pages employing four distinctly different observational lenses: theme, logic, light and delight.

Let's begin with *theme*. In recent years, in order to introduce variety to our suburban streets, Bassenian/Lagoni Architects has participated in a movement toward a more flexible residential aesthetic. A good deal of our inspiration for this comes from southern Europe. Historical antecedents in Tuscany and Andalusia respond well to very similar geographic and climatic conditions in California and the Southwest. When accepting an influence from another context, however, it is important to understand the essence of the architecture. Our aim is to apply a current translation with new-century technologies to ancient European forms and proportions and thereby "lift" the design one step further.

As a practical application, we have paid particular attention to the elements that correctly link our designs to their cultural heritage. We invite you to notice such tell-tale items as forms, details, features and colors that convey the fundamental nature of the structure (the special sections entitled "It's In the Details" will be a help). This architectural connection to the past lends a needed sense of substance and permanence and adds a frame of reference that conveys comfort and stability in an era of change and uncertainty. More importantly, look for the novel techniques and conveniences that transform an ancient aesthetic to current terms and demonstrate an evolution that has occurred over the design of a thousand homes.

Next, let's consider *logic*. At first viewing, these homes may appear oversized and more complex than their smaller and simpler predecessors. Look again. The prevailing philosophy remains consistent, bound by an understanding of the relationship of the owner to the home and the life experiences that go on there. We have incorporated "lifestyle," not just "style," into the overall design and personality of each home. In addition, these larger and well-amenitized houses are designed to forecast and stay one step ahead of the owner's needs for tomorrow.

And, look for the inherent but clearly responsive logic that promotes livability. Notice the deliberate placement of the pieces, the simplicity of the circulation, and the movement of the sight lines. Look for balance in the allocation of the spaces and in the way that each room is appropriately sized for furniture placement and usability. Sculptural playfulness is a major part of today's architectural vocabulary, so look for variety of forms and modulation of the volumes. The variation in ceiling heights must be purposeful to add surprise to the sequential experiences that unfold. Zoning between the public and private realm is important, as is the separation between formal and informal areas, and living and sleeping areas. More than ever before, the casual living area, including the kitchen, nook and family room, is where true living takes place today, so the informal realm is emphasized in these designs.

Next, look for the one element that distinguishes these homes from their 20th-century predecessors: the ambient presence of *light*. The courtyard has now been re-discovered, and it facilitates an explosion of natural light in the core of our homes. Natural light, of course, is the life force that amplifies and invigorates everything that it touches, and we have carefully designed each zone of the home to be affected and animated by its energy. The courtyard, especially, helps blur the distinction between indoors and out and is a major focal point of these houses.

As you browse this book and figuratively walk through our homes, observe how light is introduced in conventional and, on occasion, unusual ways. Patterns of light often appear as ephemeral rhythms that simply enhance the composition. In other applications, light displays usher in a spatial crescendo that illuminates a point of interest. Natural light expands and activates the visual dimensions of a home. We have devoted much thought and time to the introduction and placement of light-gathering elements because, in the final analysis, we believe that natural light gives a home its soul.

Finally, *delight* is the very necessary intangible. After all, a home should elicit excitement, feel good and lift your spirits as you come home to it and dwell in it. We believe that, in part, this pleasure comes from comfortable proportions and a clear sense of harmony. A house must display order, cleanliness of line and an architectural attitude that is in keeping with its environment—and in concert with the personality of its owner.

Yet, beyond order, purity and architectural resonance, a home must include whimsy. A house that ignites the owner's imagination can inspire ideas beyond the buzz of everyday life, reflect the uniqueness of one's own character and offer the elements of unpredictability and surprise to every first-time viewer. This is the essence of architecture—not just to shelter, but to excite, please and delight.

With this new perspective and imagery, leaf slowly through these pages, reflect, fantasize and, above all, enjoy the journey. We hope that along the way, among other reactions, you will be simply delighted.

CHAPTER ONE

TUSCAN
REFLECTIONS

The Cortile Collection
at The Bridges

Nestled high on a ridge overlooking the gently rolling hills of Rancho Santa Fe, the rugged façade of this Tuscan design evokes the primal character of a 15th-century farmhouse surrounded by the agrarian landscape of southern Italy. A rough-faced stone turret sentinels the front of the plan like an ancient bastion, establishing a dominant element above the entry. The fractured elevation conveys a pleasing transition of structural forms, which, in medieval *maisons*, were evolved over time. Rows of stone-clad clerestory windows permit natural light to pour through the single-level interior, while creating the illusion of a two-story plan at the streetscape. Set mainly in weathered brick, the tall, narrow windows of the forward gable and turret transform a rough stone wall into a point of aesthetic interest. Decorative tile vents, wrought-iron fixtures and hand-finished masonry denote the architectural genre and complement durable, low-maintenance materials that are fully prepared for the occasional extremes of the southern California climate.

A highly developed exterior vocabulary conceals the home's focus on function, flow and clarity. An I-shaped footprint performs exceptionally well in integrating the interior with the outdoors. Indoor areas activated by their visual relationship to the courtyards express the underlying emphasis on simplicity and respect for nature. Unfettered galleries that run the length and width of the house belie a network of modern essentials woven into deeply comfortable spaces.

Located just a few miles from the Pacific Ocean, this home assumes a quiet air of serenity clearly derived from its Mediterranean antecedents. The design retains the humble character of its origins while maintaining a spirit of elegance expressed by deep eaves, well-scaled masses and a smooth stucco and rough stone exterior. An ageless blend of bold rectilinear shapes and primal materials anchored by an entry turret and courtyard convey a street presence that is both pedestrian-friendly and substantial. Flexible rooms throughout the home take on everyday functions as easily as traditional events. At the core of the plan, the open living and dining rooms mix an elegant formal scale with a sense of the outdoors, creating a place where guests feel at home. French doors lead outside to a loggia and courtyard that also links the living area and the master suite, blurring the boundaries between informal and public spaces.

BUILDER: **HCC INVESTORS/LENNAR COMMUNITIES**
LOCATION: RANCHO SANTA FE, CALIFORNIA

PHOTOGRAPHY: **ERIC FIGGE**

About The Floor Plan: Design elements influenced by the rural styles of Tuscany engage flexible living zones with a deep level of comfort. Restrained by pure geometry, the open interior integrates axially related sight lines that permit wide views of nature. The entry vestibule and foyer announce a progression of spaces that lead into the plan and offer an easy transition from the streetscape. Right and left courtyards flank the core of the footprint and activate the public realm with natural light from both sides. A system of timber trusses pares down the volume in the central arena. Spare lines, unruffled textiles, aged cabinets and a subdued palette of earthen hues permit an intimate scale.

Two series of French doors line the perimeter and open to the side courtyards via a loggia and interior gallery that link to the casual living zone. Private wings wrap the left court, large enough to include a pool and spa, plenty of sitting space and an alfresco kitchen. Designed to provide varied experiences throughout the interior, the plan interposes volume with long vistas and extended sight lines. To the front of the plan, a secluded library with a centered fireplace converts to a home office and features four windows that add a greater sense of space and light. The plan's simplicity is most evident in the family room, nook and kitchen, where panels of glass and French doors permit a sense of the outdoors. A transitional space defines the approach to the owners' suite, which achieves an intimate scale by balancing exterior views with the warmth of a beamed ceiling and hardwood floors.

Previous Page | Elemental materials, varied rooflines and broken massing create a gracious, human-scaled elevation, invigorated by textured planes, deeply recessed windows and a bold tower that harbors the entry.

Opposite Page | Outcroppings of rocks, integrated into the softscapes surrounding the pool and spa area, address the alfresco living and dining area of the left courtyard. French doors open to the outside retreat from the master suite, great room and guest quarters.

4,385 SQUARE FEET

1 Entry Courtyard	9 Bedroom	17 Nook
2 Entry	10 Bathroom	18 Family Room
3 Foyer	11 Gallery Hall	19 Butler's Pantry
4 Library	12 Living Room	20 Master Bedroom
5 Casita	13 Dining Room	21 Master Bathroom
6 Wine Room	14 Loggia	22 Garage
7 Powder Room	15 Courtyard	
8 Laundry	16 Kitchen	

Above | A wall of windows brings in a sense of the outdoors that is compatible with the bold motifs of the family room and kitchen. Classic, elemental textiles mingle with pristine lines and rustic colors and develop the aesthetic presence of the room.

Opposite Page | Four sets of French doors in the central living and dining room create a fluid boundary with the left courtyard—an extensive garden anchored by a wide loggia—which includes space for alfresco meals.

It's In The
Details

Terracotta Tile, Wood & Masonry

A careful use of color, texture and scale calls up the essence of Tuscan farmhouses rooted in the rocky outcroppings and lush chaparral of the Mediterranean region. Medieval Italian houses, built from the craggy fieldstones closest at hand on primitive land stretching from Lucca to the Maremma plains, evolved over generations to high-country manors layered with tactile surfaces. Designed to outlast generations of owners, the austere country villas of the Siena plains integrated stone and brick with stucco to create durable façades that are engaged with their environments as natural extensions of the landscape.

In today's translations, rugged stone walls combine with wood and masonry elements to create appealing contrasts to the refined accoutrements of the interior. A predominant feature of the architecture then and now, reddish-orange—or terracotta—brick is used to heighten the visual effect, enrich the textured planes of the elevation and establish palatable links to the past. Sienna-hued wood lintels, beveled window trim, rafter tails purposely shaped to character and lyrically scrolled brackets iterate organic rhythms and evoke a sense of warmth and serenity. A varied terracotta-tile roof, using a flat, lipped pantile and layers of overlapping hip pantiles, create a series of ridges that extend from the eaves to the top of the roof. The archetypal elements produce an effect of sobriety and strength that firmly establishes the home in the derivative rural styles of Tuscany.

Unity is achieved in Residence One through the use of building materials that impart a strong sense of symmetry and create a visual dialogue with the southern California terrain. Terracotta bricks frame the deep recesses of the elevation, emphasizing the placement of doors and windows. Narrow arches, delineated with brick, evoke the pristine passageways of early houses nested on vast pastoral plains. Wood lintels create the effect of brows set above tall, rectilinear windows that punctuate the stone façade. Multi-paned glass doors trimmed in wood achieve links to ageless structures yet easily translate to modern motifs. The layered exterior conveys the influence of centuries-old processes adapted to fit the aesthetic requirements of the present day, and indicates the high level of artisanship found throughout the home.

Below | Cloud-white marble countertops offset the rough-hewn texture and dark hues of cabinetry built into the master bath. An enclosed tub and a step-in shower adjoin separate vanity areas and offer private garden views.

Above | Rich fabrics, bold hues and fervent blends of textures subdue wide views brought into the master bedroom through French doors—which lead out to a pool and spa area—on one side and windows that open to the golf course on the other.

Above Left | Bold earthen tones—from dark sienna to the spun-gold yellow ochre of fields of wheat—achieve a true Tuscan palette in the kitchen. The food-preparation space adjoins a quiet morning room, where only the scenery intrudes.

Above Right | A rough-hewn stone surround harbors a six-burner cooktop, one of many sleek, stainless-steel appliances that update the period accoutrements in the kitchen. Sculpted arches frame a hall pantry and gallery that adjoin the formal dining room.

Above | A view of the left courtyard reveals a rich mix of exterior surfaces and the ease with which interior space is opened gracefully to the patio.

Opposite Page | Flowerbeds, native shrubs and trees line the more intimate courtyard to the right of the plan. Clerestory windows help to diminish the scale of the stone-clad elevation and create an inviting backdrop for this outdoor retreat.

The Cortile Collection
at The Bridges

Carved into the hillside as though it were a dramatic outcrop of the native terrain, this impressive Tuscan elevation evokes the presence of a rural Italian manor. Picturesque stone walls bear witness to an architecture that goes back hundreds of years, when rich blends of renaissance dialects shaped the look of houses. Surrounded by lush, varied softscapes that call up the textured plains of Chianti and Maremma, the house is situated squarely on the site, with a symmetrical layout that is oriented toward the rear of the plan.

The formality of the entry is articulated by a bold cast-concrete surround which sets off a rough-hewn paneled door leading to an open portal. An inviting progression of spaces begins with a deep-set loggia, which wraps the central courtyard and precisely repeats the curves of the inner gallerias. In vivid contrast to the home's historic precedents, the cozy outdoor living spaces surround trappings of the digital age: a plasma TV mounted in place of the style's traditional accoutrements—impressions of palazzos or renaissance frescos—and hidden electronics that control security, lighting and climate. Inspired by early Tuscan villas, the outside space melds seamlessly with rooms in the private realm, which are linked by an airy gallery. A side-loading garage is visible to the streetscape only as a single-level wing engaged in the symmetry of the façade. Three windows contribute to the illusion of a side gable added to the home as a livable extension.

In addition to providing storage and work space, the four-car garage features a service entrance that leads past a laundry and a powder bath to a walk-through pantry and food-preparation area of the kitchen. Beyond the courtyard, a row of French doors opens to the great room, which forms a throughway to the back property and covered porch. Simple lines and elegant furnishings express a tailored motif at the core living space, in keeping with the pared-down identity of the home. Tempering these classic elements are 21st-century amenities, such as Category Five wiring for security, remote controls and high-tech media.

BUILDER: **HCC INVESTORS/LENNAR COMMUNITIES**
LOCATION: RANCHO SANTA FE, CALIFORNIA

PHOTOGRAPHY: ERIC FIGGE

Above | A row of clerestory windows overlooks the terrace, pool and spa, which nudges the landscape at the back of the plan. Three sets of French doors link the outdoor living area to the great room.

Previous Page Left | Stone pilasters sentry the forecourt, which leads to the formal entry made grand by an arched cast-stone surround and massive paneled door.

Previous Page Right | Classic proportions set off by rows of recessed windows convey an artful translation of Roman architecture at the front of the plan.

About The Floor Plan: Two dominant structures anchor the rectilinear footprint of this formal Italian manor and call to mind the simple forms of Tuscan rural houses that evolved over generations. An expansive central courtyard serves as the primary organizing element, engaged with rows of interior windows, which, in turn, permit the living spaces to interact with outdoor views. Subtle reminders of feudal farmhouses are expressed in massive stone walls and an honest symmetry that relates organically to the site.

Integrated with the fine lines and elaborate details of later renaissance styles, the house provides an air of serenity and an ordered sequence of rooms that flex according the owners' preferences. The outside-in arrangement of spaces permits public and private realms to overlap without interfering with a requisite approach to livability and comfort. Two primary structures frame the atrium, flanked by lower wings—drawn to recall single-story extensions—providing highly functional casual zones and increasing the circulation of the whole interior. The effect is one of seamless transitions—from sunlit arenas to well-scaled rooms and back again—that offer visual respite within careful integrations of bold and neutral spaces.

4,926 SQUARE FEET

1 Entry Courtyard
2 Entry Portal
3 Casita
4 Loggia
5 Courtyard
6 Gallery Hall
7 Living Room
8 Dining Room
9 Kitchen
10 Morning Room
11 Powder Room
12 Family/Media Room
13 Pantry
14 Wine Room
15 Media Closet
16 Master Bedroom
17 Master Bathroom
18 Covered Patio
19 Library/Bedroom
20 Bedroom
21 Bathroom
22 Garage
23 Laundry

Above | Viewed from the entry portal, the central courtyard offers a private sanctuary bathed in sunlight and softened by flowering plants and climbing vines.

Opposite Page | Cloud-white furnishings warm the sitting areas of the central courtyard. Massive columns define the perimeter of the space, anchored by an alfresco fireplace.

It's In The Details

Rustic Wood, Stone & Iron

A varied palette of rich textures brings a sense of the architecture of Tuscan hilltowns to this courtyard villa. A litany of native materials speaks of early rural Italian sources—with a picturesque elevation that melds dark woods with the mellow beiges and burnt-orange hues of terracotta tiles covering the roofs. Primal elements are simpatico with carefully chosen plants surrounding the modern villa, and counter the mix of über-luxe materials and styles integrated into the plan.

Rectangular moldings, tall muntin windows and faux-limestone trim underscore the simplicity of the design and enhance its elegantly rough qualities. A series of square arches leading to the four-car garage articulates the linear proportions of the stone façade, which contrasts with the pebble hues of acid-washed plaster. Carved wood cornices and curved brackets create a natural link between the built environment and the surrounding terrain, and echo the simplicity of the high timber beams of the interior. Wrought-iron brackets and metal studs fortify rough-hewn wooden entry gates inspired by medieval portals, while working shutters repeat the elemental theme.

Contrasts are employed throughout the design, with tactile surfaces—both coarse and smooth—offering an interesting balance of earthy and sophisticated elements. Rustic hearth surrounds and wax-finished fieldstone floors inside the home reflect the rich brew of materials used outdoors. The use of wood on the elevation strengthens the home's sense of rugged authenticity. Smooth stucco walls lend an urbane, tailored look to the single-level wings of the plan, and offset the intense hues of the forward gable with muted shades of ochre and sand.

Opposite Page | Paneled walls and hardwood floors add character to the guest casita, a secluded, contained space that easily converts to a home office.

Below |The owners' bath boasts a tropical shower with separate drying areas that frames a spa-style tub with an elegant marble surround.

Above | Deep indigo and pine hues enliven the restrained architecture of the master bedroom, a private retreat where only daylight and scenery are permitted entry.

Previous Page Left |Warm Mediterranean hues link the courtyard with the great room, which opens to outside living spaces on both sides through French doors.

Previous Page Right | Beamed ceilings and clerestory windows add dimension to an open arrangement of the formal dining room and kitchen.

Above | Just outside of the great room, a *plein air* space features an outdoor bar and sitting area sheltered by the loggia. Stone pavers unify the extended zone and complement the palette of natural materials used throughout the home.

Opposite Page | Five clerestory windows contribute to a two-story presentation at the rear perimeter and permit natural light to illuminate the great room. A series of French doors lead to a covered porch and an outer living area that achieves a sense of unity with native plants and materials.

Canyon's Edge
at Turtle Ridge

In a break with tradition, these Tuscan-style homes address the street with simple, well-articulated forms that are not grand or monumental but reserved and fashionable. Designed for an innovative cluster community in the foothills near Turtle Rock Village in Irvine, California, these village-scaled residences offer flexible indoor environments and fluid links to outside spaces. Thick stone-clad walls, clay-tile roofs and rough-hewn stone turrets evoke the rustic character of Tuscan farmhouses and create a sense of informality. Layered massing conveys the varied scale of each plan and enhances the more compact component of the paired footprints.

Residence Two transforms the project into a collaborative community, with an L-shaped plan that wraps Residence Three and provides opportunities for private courtyards and exclusive outdoor living areas. The fractured façade conceals an adaptable floor plan with flexible options for the upper and lower levels. Just off the entry, a secluded den easily converts to a study, home office or guest room. French doors open the service hall to a private courtyard. The casual living space flexes from public to private, with an open link to the kitchen that invites small family gatherings or a huge bash. An upper-level bonus room can be developed to accommodate guests.

Residence Three's simplicity is the key to this highly functional home. A tiled entry vestibule connects the foyer with the main stairs and leads to a flexible space that converts to a home office, library or master suite. To the right of the foyer, the airy living and dining room provides a fireplace and a media niche. The food-preparation area of the kitchen overlooks the central living space, creating an unrestrained geometry conducive to entertaining. Upstairs, two large bedroom suites are easily converted to an owners' retreat and guest quarters.

BUILDER: **STANDARD PACIFIC HOMES**
LOCATION: IRVINE, CALIFORNIA

PHOTOGRAPHY: **LANCE GORDON**

About The Floor Plan: With the character of a small European village, the development sustains a spirit of informality and, through an organic composition enriched by a range of earthen hues, manages to blend back into the canyon environment. Walkable streets and pedestrian-friendly ways establish an inviting atmosphere in the scenic village. Clusters of single-family homes designed primarily for an age-targeted market of empty-nesters offer ground-floor master suites and flexible informal spaces. Well-positioned entries and refined outer living areas permit both privacy and a sense of community in this new-century neighborhood. French doors allow access to courtyard settings and open the plans to natural light. Arranged in pairs, Residences Two and Three create a symbiotic unity with well-matched perimeters that maintain a sense of seclusion and maximize the livability of both plans. With an intentionally wide footprint, Plan Two offers a more luxurious disposition with an extensive presentation to the street.

1 Entry	9 Powder Room
2 Parlor	10 Laundry
3 Living Room	11 Garage
4 Dining Room	12 Courtyard
5 Kitchen	13 Master Bedroom
6 Great Room	14 Master Bathroom
7 Bedroom/Second Master	15 Retreat
8 Bathroom	16 Bedroom/Retreat/Office

Previous Page Left | Residence Three offers a massive stone entry tower, which houses a winding staircase linking the upper and lower levels. Twin windows, separated by a pilaster, evoke reflections from the past.

Previous Page Right | Trees and landscape line the outer spaces of Residence Two, which features a forecourt and a recessed entry harbored by a center turret. Stone and smooth stucco add contrasting textures to the informal elevation.

Second Floor

First Floor

Site Plan

SITE PLAN GRAPHIC:
AARON MARTINEZ

About The Site Plan: Located on an idyllic site in the arcadian foothills of Turtle Ridge in Irvine, this project strategically positions the clusters of plans to maximize use of the view-studded property. Perimeters of the homes are designed with increased fenestration that permits plenty of natural light inside.

Cluster Plan

About The Cluster Plan: Interlocking lots allow opportunities for courtyard environments and outside living areas that promote a feeling of privacy and maintain the owners' autonomy within the clustered community. Residence Two features an L-shaped plan that wraps the more compact Residence Three with a two-story elevation.

Above | In Residence Three, the convenient arrangement of the kitchen and flexible living and dining area features a fireplace and media center that warms the ambience of the entire space. Overhead decorative beams offer a sense of intimacy and accentuate the informal quality of the style.

Below | Euro-style white cabinetry features raised-panel doors in Residence One's well-organized kitchen, which opens to the dining and living area (floor plan not shown). The space flexes to a public zone for entertaining, with a food-preparation counter that converts to a buffet.

Above | Shallow-profiled trusses cap Residence Two's open arrangement of the central living area and kitchen, positioned near the formal dining room. Sleek, stainless-steel appliances play harmony with crafted cabinetry in the kitchen, anchored by a curved snack counter that is designed to increase food-preparation space and storage.

DeFelice Residence
at Shady Canyon

In the softly green rolling hills of Shady Canyon, this unpretentious courtyard villa employs hand-set stone to meld the forward gables of its façade into the scenery. Thick masonry walls, stone floors, multi-level massing and coarse timbers offset patterned brick lintels that articulate the structure of the residence. Toward the street, the farmhouse architecture purposely draws the eye to a deeply recessed arched entry, which opens at once to a large central courtyard that transforms the scale of the home. The visual impact at entry is softened by the rich earthen tones and rustic textures of the covered portico, which is defined by the rough-hewn beams, exposed clay tile and rigorous architecture of the arcade. A processional experience through the courtyard to the two-story structure imposes an element of surprise that is repeated in the thoughtful progression of space that unfolds throughout the home. The architect's intent is evident in the asymmetrical massing, gracefully sculpted arches and understated tone of the whole interior. A fluid composition of indoors and out, the plan conveys the venerable character of its historic informal antecedents, with human-scaled rooms and elegant galleries that house the owners' sizeable art collection. Works by contemporary artists add points of interest to the termini of sight lines, while individual elements—such as the courtyard herringbone pavers and the imported cast fireplace in the living room—affirm the authenticity of the design.

BUILDER: **WARMINGTON CUSTOM HOMES**
LOCATION: IRVINE, CALIFORNIA

PHOTOGRAPHY: ERIC FIGGE

About The Floor Plan: A handcrafted stone walkway leads through an entry gate to a covered portico overlooking the central courtyard. Defined by a colonnade of arches, the gallery forms an axial relationship with the private wings of the home, and offers a transition to the two-story structure beyond the courtyard. The true entry—a massive, oak-paneled door—translates the idyllic experience of the outer zone into a cultivated formal space that is central to the pace of the whole house. At the heart of the plan, the living and dining room receives natural light from both the courtyard and rear loggia—which shelters the rooms from the sun—and offers a view of the grounds through three sets of French doors.

The casual living area, including the kitchen, morning nook and family room, assumes a less dominant yet equally strategic position to the right of the plan. A triple window takes in vistas of the lush property, and a rotunda serves as a passageway to a service hall and a home office. Upstairs, the master suite includes a spacious den/retreat with a fireplace, and a gallery hall that leads to a study and out to a covered balcony that allows views of the surrounding hills.

Above | Imported from Tuscany, the massive cast fireplace with its handcarved pilasters contrasts with rugged timber beams in the living room. French doors bring in daylight from both the rear loggia and courtyard, while twin arches provide passageways to a private wing, which includes a library.

Below | In the master bedroom, a plank ceiling hovers above a textured palette of furnishings infused with vivid hues and rich fabrics. Near the arch-top window, a French door leads to a private deck.

Previous Page Left | Shrouded by olive groves and sentried by two fieldstone piers, the elevation captures the spirit of an ancient farmhouse. Multi-level massing and pleasing juxtapositions of rustic and refined elements add contemporary vitality to the vintage façade.

Previous Page Right | Past the entry gate, the rugged textures of the portico enhance the transition to the central courtyard, which leads to the true front door. A balcony with a wrought-iron railing overlooks a wishing well and an outdoor sitting area grouped with chic gray furnishings.

6,064 SQUARE FEET

1 Entry	9 Butler's Pantry	17 Powder Room
2 Courtyard	10 Home Office	18 Wet Bar
3 Living Room	11 Laundry	19 Garage
4 Dining Room	12 Gallery Hall	20 Den/Retreat
5 Loggia	13 Bathroom	21 Deck
6 Kitchen	14 Casita	22 Master Bedroom
7 Nook	15 Bedroom	23 Master Bathroom
8 Family Room	16 Study	

Second Floor

First Floor

Above | Rugged brick pavers and rough-hewn beams define smooth planes of cream-white stucco and sleek ceramic vases rooted with vines. Wrought-iron sconces evoke the spirit of Tuscan farmhouses.

Above | On the upper level, hardwood floors unify an expansive retreat that includes a private sitting room, a study/home office and a master suite that leads to a portico. Daylight seeps into the rotunda from the owners' bedroom.

Above Left | A series of graceful arches leads past the living room and stair hall to a private vestibule bearing a contemporary work from the owners' sizeable art collection. Natural light from the central courtyard bathes the front of the home with a serene ambience.

Opposite Page | A quiet study offers space for repose, with hardwood floors and wide vistas of the rear property. Designed to flex with the lifestyles of the owners, the room converts to a home office or even guest quarters.

Above Right | Period fixtures lend a European spirit to a thoroughly modern kitchen, which features a food-preparation area that overlooks the casual living space. Granite counters and tile floor offer a pleasing contrast to rich wood cabinetry.

Above | Designed to draw people outdoors, the rear elevation offers transitional space in the upper and lower porticos. Fringed with native shrubs, the terrace steps into the terrain with a primal spirit, quietly and in sync with local wildlife.

Opposite Page | Exposed clay tiles and timber beams interpret the past at the entry gate, reinforced by modern applications of stone, brick and iron. A robust colonnade opens directly to the central courtyard, which features an outdoor fireplace.

Shady Canyon Residence

Shady Canyon, a private residential and golf preserve in Irvine, California, integrates forever-protected open space with a low-density village of eco-sensitive designs that present the informal character of rural European styles—from Southern Spain to Italy. Situated on an uphill lot, the house conforms to the natural grade and offers commanding views of the surrounding countryside. At the front of the plan, single-level elements retain the modest proportions of the earlier styles, while the elevation extends to two stories above the courtyard. The turret rises even taller to mark its presence on the hillside. The broad use of rough stone integrates the home with the rocky terrain and establishes links to nature that prevail throughout the plan.

With a practical arrangement of indoor-outdoor rooms, the design revolves around a central courtyard. Located immediately inside the foyer, the formal living room serves as a forward comfort zone and a transitional area. The gallery hall employs extended sight lines to create a dialogue with the casual realm. Along the central spine of the plan, a series of French doors opens the family room to the loggia and courtyard.

On the other side of the outdoor space, a two-sided fireplace shared with the parlor warms an alfresco sitting area. Panels of glass and rows of windows permit intricate plays of sunlight along the rear perimeter, which opens to painterly vistas of scenery through an upper portico. On the second floor, positioned above the family room, the master suite overlooks the courtyard and opens to the elements, permitting an intimate connection with the landscape. Exposed wood beams supported by simple Doric columns enhance the covered outside living space, while a forward staircase leads from the bedroom to an observation tower that harbors a sitting area offering panoramic views.

BUILDER: **WARMINGTON CUSTOM HOMES**
LOCATION: IRVINE, CALIFORNIA

PHOTOGRAPHY: ERIC FIGGE

Second Floor

Tower Plan

5,793 SQUARE FEET

1 Entry

2 Living Room

3 Gallery Hall

4 Courtyard

5 Dining Room

6 Loggia

7 Powder Room

8 Kitchen

9 Morning Room

10 Butler's Pantry

11 Family Room

12 Bedroom

13 Bathroom

14 Laundry

15 Garage

16 Master Bedroom

17 Master Bathroom

18 Deck

19 Sitting/Reading Area

20 Home Office

First Floor

Above | Simple Doric columns support a wood-beam ceiling on the covered deck that overlooks the courtyard. Tall recessed windows punctuate the rugged stone texture of the observation tower, which dominates the elevation.

Below Left and Right | Dark-stained muntin windows and doors contrast with smooth stucco and rough stone exteriors to create rich counterpoints of color and texture.

Previous Page Left | A series of sculpted arches facing the courtyard counters the rough-hewn exposed beams of the covered deck on the upper level. Clay-tile roofs and stone pavers add texture to the fractured and layered architecture.

Previous Page Right | Nested into the site and rising with the landscape as if belonging to the surrounding hills, the home employs an extensive use of stone to meld into the scenery. Single-level elements rise to two stories, and shoulder the tower that rises beyond.

It's In The
Details

Cast Concrete, Stone & Shutters

The front of the Shady Canyon Residence maintains a modest scale with single-story elements that evolve to a more complex profile toward the courtyard and back elevation. Designed to face the street with simple side gables that interlock to create the sense of a hilltown villa, the architecture achieves a crescendo at the observation tower, which hovers above the plan's layered composition of forms. As in Tuscany—where a tower often fortifies a cluster of structures—this home's architectural extension anchors the façade and marks its presence in the community.

True to the vernacular, the house employs rugged fieldstone to unify the elevation with the terrain—along the ground plane, inside the courtyard and along the walls. Around the perimeter, cast-concrete elements surround the doors and windows, tailoring the look and function of the narrow, recessed openings, and creating a logical transition between the rough stone and the finished materials. The tall vertical dimensions of the windows evoke the proportions and character of the Mediterranean region. Archetypal elements of the rural villas include fully operational shutters, which are repeated here for aesthetic as well as practical purposes.

On the covered deck above the courtyard, exposed wood beams terminate in shaped rafter tails that add texture to the weathered-stone façade. Even when the eave extension is minimized, it is detailed to offer a strong shadow line and further accentuate the masculine architecture.

Whispering Glen
at Turtle Ridge

At the heart of Orange County, this community features attached homes in varied configurations that create a highly efficient multi-family neighborhood in the city of Irvine. Set against the rolling hills of Turtle Ridge, the layered planes and asymmetrical massing of the clustered buildings convey an attitude reminiscent of groupings of villas in tranquil Tuscan hilltowns. Each structure consists of two single-level plans, or flats, which offer direct access to a private garage, and two townhomes—each placed above its own garage. As in Tuscany, vertical, tall and narrow openings mark the fenestration of the textured stucco and masonry façades. Stone cladding occurs along a central gable up to the second-floor eaves to add visual interest and reduce the scale of the structures from the street. Hip roofs decrease the vertical impact of the presentation and maintain the scale and sense of a rural village. Covered balconies absorb scenery through arched openings that add character to the exteriors, while shutters shield second-story windows from harsh, direct sunlight. Precast concrete frames accentuate the deeply recessed entries and assign individuality to the front of the home. Throughout the various floor plans, architectural amenities ease the function and flow of the whole house. Covered decks lined with large openings bring natural light and scenery into the interiors and allow enough space for outdoor seating. Halls and galleries feature built-in shelves and cabinetry that harbor computers and media equipment. Adaptable spaces convert to home offices or guest rooms, and create personal retreats for the owners.

BUILDER: **SHEA HOMES**
LOCATION: IRVINE, CALIFORNIA

PHOTOGRAPHY: **WILL HARE, JR.**

Above Top | In Plan One, a winding staircase links the second floor to an upper-level hall that leads to the master suite. Pale yellow walls and paneled white cabinetry tame the high volume of the main living space.

Above Bottom | At the core of Plan Four, the formal dining room intimately connects with the kitchen—which allows the cook to participate in conversation with guests—and opens to a covered patio. Just off the entry, a room adapts to the owners' lifestyles and provides space for guests or live-in relatives.

Previous Page Left | A layered elevation conveys a modern disposition and harbors a multi-family complex that offers both privacy and community.

Previous Page Right | A deeply recessed archway leads from a picturesque courtyard to a stairway that connects to the upper-level entry rotunda.

Third Floor

Second Floor

First Floor

Above | Within each building, a fourplex configuration composed of one-, two- and three-story elements creates playful massing at the street. Stone cladding and covered balconies add texture and interest to the façade, evoking the charm of rustic rural Tuscan villas.

Below | Invention and repetition work in tandem to effect an engaging street presentation. Vertical, narrow windows and a deeply recessed entry complement the stucco and stone exterior, offering an appealing fenestration that permits plenty of natural light.

Villa Firenze
Renaissance at Stonetree Golf Club

Nestled in the mountainous northern California terrain not far from San Pablo Bay, this captivating Tuscan elevation is inspired by the rural architecture of Italy's most scenic regions. Drawn for a hilly site, this downslope home is oriented toward the rear of the property and takes full advantage of panoramas afforded by its prime location. Stone cladding marks the exterior, adding character and a rich texture evocative of European farmhouses. Precast concrete elements surround tall windows and a recessed entry, accentuating the dominant turret, which establishes a strong street presence for the façade. At the main level, a rotunda foyer grants extended vistas of the formal dining room, and leads through French doors to a den that doubles as a home office. The living room opens to the central hall through a broad arch and links to the den via a through-fireplace. At the opposite side of the plan, the casual living zone features an angled hearth, a wet bar and a media center, with a wall of windows that lets in plenty of natural light. A central stairway leads to the lower level, which provides a recreation room, a laundry and two secondary bedrooms that share a hall bath. To the left, the rambling master suite includes a fireplace and a spacious bath with separate amenities and two walk-in closets.

BUILDER: **DAVIDON HOMES**
LOCATION: NOVATO, CALIFORNIA

PHOTOGRAPHY: **TIM MALONEY**

Opposite Page | Rough stone and smooth, contrasting stucco enjoy a definite connection to the Tuscan region, echoing the open galleries, enormous fireplaces and thick stone walls of old Tuscan farmhouses.

Lower Level

First Floor

4,505 SQUARE FEET

1 Entry
2 Home Office
3 Guest Bedroom
4 Bathroom
5 Powder Room
6 Living Room
7 Dining Room
8 Gallery Hall
9 Kitchen
10 Nook
11 Family Room
12 Garage
13 Deck
14 Game Room
15 Bedroom
16 Master Bedroom
17 Master Bathroom
18 Laundry
19 Wine Cellar

CHAPTER TWO

ANDALUSIAN
REFLECTIONS

Ultimate Family Home
Demonstration House

Sited little more than shouting distance from the bright lights of Las Vegas' animated metropolis, this sophisticated elevation expresses deeply rooted Hispanic instincts. The purposefully massed façade approaches the street with a pedestrian-friendly forecourt, which wraps the front perimeter. To the right of the formal entry, a tower harbors an arched window and establishes the design's singular presence in an enclave of semi-custom houses. Not far from the vast stretches of desert that nudge the perimeters of new residential developments, this hacienda-style home corresponds to its habitat with intimate links to the scenery. French doors lead to courtyards, patios, upper decks, water features and expanses of lawn throughout the plan—offering wide views that sometimes include glimpses of one of the world's most famous skylines.

Rough-sawn beams and rustic pavers integrate the home's indoor environment with *plein air* spaces and help create a medley of warm Mediterranean hues. Form and texture are carefully orchestrated to intimate the earthy palette of Spanish colonial retreats evolved over centuries. Mortar-set brick and plaster-finished stucco enrich the boundaries of the home, in harmony with a clay-tile roof and an authentic vocabulary of earthen tones: ochre, pebble and terracotta. Mosaic tiles inspire a villa-over-the-water disposition, adding a Moorish influence that layers historic elements with flurries of bravado. Shaped corbels, carved rafter tails and tall, recessed windows articulate the refined origins of the exterior and sustain an ethnic sensibility that is complementary to the engaging yet technically advanced accoutrements of the interior.

Designed for new-century mindsets, the house employs sustainable devices—such as photovoltaic panels and radiant-barrier sheathing under the roof tiles—as well as eco-conscious materials: the whole plan is built from certified wood harvested from growth-managed forests. Every room supports computers, the house meets zero-energy standards and the plan successfully melds innovative technology with satisfying traditional spaces.

The plan demonstrates a fluidity and high level of function uncommon to large, three-story homes, with a linear footprint designed to take advantage of the courtyard areas. The innovative home management center offers a homework area, multi-user desk and computer spaces, and links to communication and security systems.

BUILDER: **PARDEE HOMES**
LOCATION: LAS VEGAS, NEVADA

PHOTOGRAPHY: **ERIC FIGGE**

5,300 SQUARE FEET

1 Entry Courtyard	14 Walk-In Pantry	27 Tree House
2 Entry	15 Mud/Locker Room	28 Water Slide
3 Living Room	16 Laundry	29 Bedroom
4 Dining Room	17 Sport/Motor Court	30 Bathroom
5 Library/Study	18 Tool Shed	31 Master Bedroom
6 Guest Suite/Casita	19 Bicycle Storage	32 Master Bathroom
7 Loggia	20 Work Shop	33 Retreat
8 Powder Room	21 Garage	34 Deck
9 Kitchen	22 Central Courtyard	35 Book Loft
10 Nook	23 Pavillion	36 Hideaway
11 Home Management Ctr.	24 Pool Bath	37 Loft/Gameroom
12 Family Room	25 Barbeque	38 Wine Storage
13 Prep Kitchen	26 Firepit	39 Gallery Hall

First Floor

Second Floor

Third Floor

About The Floor Plan: A gated forecourt offers a strategic approach to the house, with a series of mosaic and terracotta tile stairs leading through a mid-level landing to ease the transition from the sidewalk to the formal entry. Continuity and an economy of space give the project an air of informality, with a series of unspoiled open-air environments linked to highly functional rooms. On nice days, the entire house opens to the outdoors—from the forecourt to the central courtyard and covered loggia, which surrounds a bubble-up fountain and leads to an open-air pavilion, patio kitchen and outer living zone. The entry serves as a transition space between the formal rooms, yet maintains its own identity with fluid links to the front and back properties. French doors connect the public realm with the courtyards and an arched window brings in natural light. In the living room, dual passageways flank the fireplace and lead to a flexible study that opens to the outdoors on both sides. A private vestibule announces the guest wing, a flexible suite that converts to a downstairs master suite as the owners' lifestyles change.

At the core of the plan, the family center includes an innovative home management area, which provides a multi-user desk and computer spaces with high-speed internet access, and a command station that helps monitor energy usage and security. The gourmet kitchen boasts ergonomic fixtures—including wireless light dimmers and digital readouts—with a food-preparation counter that morphs daily to a project table for homework. Nearby, a prep kitchen handles easy meals and converts to a servery for planned events. A utility hall leads to a mud room, where individual lockers contain the family's personal gear and pets have their own space as well. On the second level, the children's bedrooms are equipped with compartmented baths. A hideaway room with a secret door invites video karaoke sessions. An airy master retreat features a flexible sitting area—a space that can serve as a den or nursery—while a tropical shower highlights the owners' bath. The third-floor loft, used as a game room, offers its own plasma television, plus space for books and computers. A series of tall windows brokers sunlight that illuminates the space and grants spectacular views of the city.

Previous Page | An artful combination of terracotta brick and sand-colored stucco adds texture and warmth to the well-balanced proportions of the hacienda-like elevation.

Above | Employing the elements of layering and accentuated scale, the elevation surges toward the Nevada sky at its center and subtly approaches the sidewalk from the formal entry. Hispanic origins are evident in a boosted clay-tile roof, shaped corbels, carved rafter tails and rows of recessed windows.

Below | Two- and three-story elements vary the visual dimensions of the central courtyard, enhanced by lush outcroppings of verdant growth. An extensive covered loggia eases access to the outside from the family center, dining and living rooms, entry and study.

Above | French doors and glass panels let in plenty of natural light, illuminating the formal dining room. Dark-stained timbers enrich the shaped drywall stairs leading to the third-level loft, visually linking the stairway to the beamed ceiling. Wrought-iron fixtures interact with the ornamented balusters of the balcony and stair rails.

Opposite Page | Defined by a textured brick arch that borders the entry, the dining room conveys a sense of grandeur. The sculpted stairway to the upper level adds aesthetic impact and harbors a wine closet tucked beneath it. In the soaring formal rooms, natural light plays over a mix of materials.

It's In The Details

The Ultimate Family Center

At the center of the home, sight lines and vistas extend the visual dimensions of the highly functional kitchen, family room and home management center—a computerized hub that provides homework stations for the kids, and monitors energy usage, home security and the family calendar. Two laptops, a scheduling board and plenty of cabinet space ease everyday tasks, and help to organize the chaotic whir of activities and scheduled events. An exact mirror of the nook space, the management center is equipped with a built-in display that permits owners to monitor the zero-energy home's kilowatt production generated by photovoltaic panels on the home's south side.

Mocha-glazed maple cabinetry, granite countertops and cast-stone elements achieve a casual elegance that complements the sleek, techno-savvy character of the whole house. The central food-preparation island is appropriately scaled for the kitchen's generous square footage, with enough counter space for impromptu snacks and science projects. Nearby, a prep kitchen provides a place for event planning, catering and party preparation, and features lower-height appliances and child-friendly amenities that permit easy access to cool beverages and after-school treats.

A confluence of outdoor views infuses the central spaces with daylight and scenery. Two large arched windows—in the family room and the morning nook—frame the axis points for the informal wing and engage the interior with courtyard vistas and a spirit of nature. The cruciform shape of the family center creates a cluster of intimate spaces offset by the voluminous family and media room, which serves as the audio and visual distribution center for the home. Plenty of windows extend sight lines to the outer property and reveal glimpses of playful backyard spaces, including the fire pit, water slide and treehouse.

Above | Massive square brick columns line the edge of the loggia and offer an airy boundary to the central court-yard. To the rear of the plan, a French door leads to a secluded guest suite.

Opposite Page | An open-air pavilion is equipped with three television screens and access to the interior's audio and visual feeds. Fully furnished around a gas fireplace, this outdoor living room adjoins an alfresco kitchen and the swimming pool.

Above | Mosaic tiles enliven the Moorish-influenced fountain surround in the forecourt—a transitional space dominated by a three-story tower. The playful elevation overlooks a pleasing progression through the courtyard from the sidewalk to the formal entry.

Above | Stone pavers line the terrace surrounding the pool and spa area, offering a link to the natural terrain. Nearby, a jungle treehouse, bridge lookout and water slide create an adventure zone for children.

The Sycamores
at Shady Canyon

Influenced by the courtyard houses of rural Andalusia, this revival design encourages an enjoyment of Orange County's Mediterranean-style climate and establishes a series of satisfying connections between the interior and outside living areas. Layered massing conveys a sense of history and articulates the varied architecture of early houses, which evolved over time. True to the vernacular, the home makes an immediate presentation to the street and offers the impact of a two-story structure, while the interior provides the convenience of a single-level home. A dentil frieze, cast-concrete doorway and clay roof tiles enrich the front elevation, which is finished with slurried, rough-textured masonry, reflecting the rugged brick exteriors of Andalusian retreats. Deeply recessed windows, ornamented arches, decorative tiles and intricately detailed brackets accentuate the design and complement the hacienda feel of the structure. Triple walls pene-

trated by an entry door, a narrow hallway, an intimate forecourt and then a formal entry provide a progressive experience from the porch to the central courtyard. Dramatic sculpted arches announce the rich character of the home, which proceeds around the courtyard, permitting natural light to activate the interior. Form follows function as the house progresses from the well-defined formal rooms to the more flexible spaces of the casual living zone. French doors and wide panels of glass permit views to pervade the forward plan—a mix of public and private spaces—which includes a casita and a guest suite. At the edge of the public wing, adjoining the great room, the library serves as a transitional space linking the outside area with the owners' retreat, and flexing from a parlor or conversation room to a comfortable space for study and repose. The rear hall links the great room to a spacious loggia, which eases the transition to the outside.

BUILDER: **GREYSTONE HOMES—A LENNAR COMPANY**
LOCATION: IRVINE, CALIFORNIA

PHOTOGRAPHY: ERIC FIGGE

4,097 SQUARE FEET

1 Breezeway Entry	9 Dining Room	17 Gallery Hall
2 Entry Courtyard	10 Morning Room	18 Master Bedroom
3 Entry	11 Laundry	19 Retreat
4 Courtyard	12 Powder Room	20 Master Bathroom
5 Great Room	13 Home Office/Library	21 Loggia
6 Kitchen	14 Bedroom	22 Garage
7 Dirty/Working Kitchen	15 Bathroom	
8 Butler's Pantry	16 Casita	

About The Floor Plan: From the entry, the house unfolds sequentially around the courtyard in a series of rooms that proceed from public to private realms. Varied vertical masses achieve a dynamic progression of spaces, with dimensions that fluctuate between modest and impressive. Natural light comes between the forms, activating the inside spaces and giving the entire home an airy, informal character. A highly sophisticated arrangement of rooms with varying ceiling heights offsets wide-open spaces with areas tailored to a more human scale. High-volume living areas, such as the great room, satisfy a requirement for increased visual dimensions in the public spaces and maintain an elevated sense of aesthetics. Single-story building forms with reduced vertical volume harbor the intimate living areas of the private sphere, with modest proportions that complement the grand, vaulted spaces of the home.

Elements of surprise enrich the interior, such as a formal dining room that provides flow across the central gallery to the primary courtyard. At the front of the plan, the forecourt opens to a grand interior vista that extends through the entry vestibule to the outdoor living zone, which leads back inside to the great room. A flexible arrangement of rooms at the entry permits the casita's primary suite to convert to a home office. A secluded library activated by access to the courtyard connects axially to the rear gallery hall—a transitional space that leads to the loggia and the rear property. The master retreat also opens to the outdoors, with controlled yet open links to the casual living zone.

Opposite Page | From the central courtyard, the entry and forecourt lead to the breezeway entry, an intimate space linking the home with the outer terrace and sidewalk. Pebble-colored masonry walls complement massive knotty-alder paneled doors and the traditional terracotta tones of the brick pavers.

Previous Page Left | The architectural ingenuity of the plan is revealed at the streetscape, with a rambling Spanish façade that is anchored by a central entry element that ascends to a two-story height.

Previous Page Right | Brick pavers line the steps and forecourt that lead into the home, easing the transition from the sidewalk to the formal entry. A detailed dentil frieze adds texture to the masonry façade, and sculpted precast forms announce the grandeur of the plan.

Above Left | Bold shapes and high timber trusses give definition to the vaulted great room and a wide-open kitchen. Dual passageways lead to a more compact service space, where a food-preparation area facilitates planned meals and traditional events.

Above Right | In the formal dining room, an arched window echoes the curve of the opening that defines the inner perimeter of the space. Ceramic tile offers a sense of unity with the kitchen, accessed through a butler's pantry.

Opposite Page | An arched opening frames the morning room, where a centered window extends the site lines to outdoor vistas and French doors open to the loggia.

It's In The Details

Cast Concrete, Brick & Iron

A simplified sculpted surround of precast concrete indicates the Andalusian origins of the masonry façade. The solid, uninterrupted plane of the street presentation expresses the straightforwardness of the design, with references to the home's primal Hispanic roots. Below the roofline, a dentil band and ornamented frieze break the massive scale of the forward structure, which is composed of slurried brick. The Romans were the first to use the pebble-grey hues—limestone blocks were known to be quarried by them in medieval and renaissance times—employing huge blocks of stone to create a smooth or decorated surface. The layering of building materials, originally intended to fortify the structure, became a technique employed to infuse the elevation with a weathered look. On rural villas and houses, touches of brickwork added a sense of refinement above a doorway or along the brow of a window.

Here the masonry evokes the raw ruggedness of provincial structures, yet takes on a thoroughly modern theme, adding subtle definition and interest to impart a sense of harmony to the elevation. The texture, pattern and color of the slurried brick create a distinctive ornamentation to the front of the home. Even a simple window covering takes on an elegant appearance with the addition of a decorative wrought-iron grille. Ornamental detail is key to the Andalusian scheme, with balustrades, posts and sconces fashioned to complement the rough-textured materials of the home's exterior. Delicate finials and scrolls define the character of the ironwork and contribute significantly to the appeal of the home from the street.

Above | Sun and shadow are an integral part of the architecture throughout the home, and especially at the central courtyard. French doors and large panels of glass blur the boundaries between indoors and out, and permit natural light and breezes to mingle with the furnishings inside.

Opposite Page | Deeply carved timber beams and rows of clerestory windows subdue the volume of the great room. Natural light adds a sense of the outdoors to the interior and activates the rooms with views to the courtyard.

The Cortile Collection
at The Bridges

Reflecting 15th-century Andalusian architecture, this refined elevation combines the elegance of sculpted cast forms and modeled plaster with slurried masonry and terracotta-tile roofs. Layered panels, deeply recessed doors and windows, and varied rooflines accentuate the fractured façade, which establishes an unusual yet distinctive street presence. An idiosyncratic entresol cantilevers above a graceful rusticated arch that harbors the breezeway, entry portico and forecourt. A progressive approach to the formal entry eases the transition from the sidewalk through a public vestibule to an airy succession of interior galleries and well-scaled rooms that receive natural light from the spacious central courtyard. Hispanic influences abound—earthen-hued stone floors, heavy roof trusses, recessed clerestories and rustic hearths—in both the great room and the center courtyard. Understated furnishings iterate the purity of the motif, with simple forms and rough-hewn textures that emphasize the honesty of the structure. In keeping with an authentic vocabulary, the function-conscious layout pares away extraneous details and engenders the plan with free-flowing spaces that flex and change with current lifestyles. An optional den near the entry converts to a guest suite and provides access to the main courtyard from the central gallery. A spacious library extends the livability of the master wing and creates a fluid boundary between the loggia and central courtyard. A connected casita becomes a private home office or provides accommodations for an au pair or live-in relative. Throughout the home, inner spaces meld into outer zones, extending the spatial and visual boundaries of the rooms. A long, broad patio wraps around the hill side of the home, translating the rugged scenery of the surrounding terrain into a refined series of softscapes that are compatible with the mood and materials of an urbane interior.

BUILDER: **HCC INVESTORS/LENNAR COMMUNITIES**
LOCATION: RANCHO SANTA FE, CALIFORNIA

PHOTOGRAPHY: ERIC FIGGE

4,374 SQUARE FEET

1 Entry Breezeway

2 Entry Courtyard

3 Entry

4 Courtyard

5 Great Room

6 Kitchen

7 Dirty/Working Kitchen

8 Butler's Pantry

9 Dining Room

10 Wine Room

11 Powder Room

12 Laundry

13 Morning Room

14 Wet Bar

15 Hall

16 Library/Media Room

17 Master Bedroom

18 Master Bathroom

19 Bedroom/Home Office

20 Bedroom

21 Bathroom

22 Loggia

23 Casita

24 Garage

Above | Wide terracotta stairs offer a progressive experience leading from ground level to the elevated forecourt and formal entry. Lush landscaping enhances the walkway, capturing the beauty of terraced plant life typifying Andalusian villas.

Previous Page Left | A vernacular style of the Andalusian region features a clay-tile shed roof and a prominent forward gable. The projecting bay hovers above a deeply recessed entry with a cast-stone surround.

Previous Page Right | Arcadian softscapes flank the pedestrian-friendly path leading to the home's main entry. The textured façade derives its serene beauty from a variety of elements—slurried masonry, stucco and clay-tile roofs—characteristic of the dialects of southern Spain.

About The Floor Plan: The design makes perfect use of a centuries-old tradition drawn from the rural architecture of southern Spain, employing a sloped roof and a recessed entry that is designed to offer shelter from the sun. Lively variations in the layered forms lend an exuberant spirit to the elevation, which responds to the rugged terrain with a tactile, richly textured façade. The plan groups a cluster of interior spaces around the central courtyard—a significant reference to the fortified *cortijo* houses of Andalusia. Open, airy living spaces are linked to the outside zones by rows of French doors that amplify a sense of nature inside.

The careful sequence of rooms provides a progressive experience through the home, with fluid transitions from well-scaled galleries and shapely niches to the great outdoors. The great room effects a successful transition from the central courtyard—which is set off by rows of French doors linking public and private rooms—to the tranquility of the rear loggia. Terraced gardens surround a pool and spa area, and lend a sense of formality to the outdoor zone. The basic symmetry of the plan is masked by a series of varied approaches to the outdoor center of the home, and a fluid progression of spaces that flex from formal to casual.

Opposite Page | A succession of courts leads from the sidewalk to the entry of the home, anchored by a breezy portico and fountain. Sculpted cast-stone surrounds create an inviting arcade that progresses through both grand and intimate spaces.

Above | The formal entry grants stunning vistas of the forecourt and portico, and provides a transition to the home's gracious interior. A corridor to the central courtyard links the main gallery hall to guest quarters and a flex room that leads outside.

It's In The
Details

Terracotta and Mosaic Tile

This idyllic outdoor sanctuary is formed through a detailed loggia that serves as a fluid extension of the private gallery lining the casual living zone. Lush swaths of olive trees, palms and citrus cut into the rolling hills surrounding the property, and create an easy bond with the varied softscapes of the perimeter. The villa's timeless character imbues the *plein air* spaces with a sense of the past, vividly expressed by the lively composition of bold, shapely forms and rough-hewn textures. Picturesque massing combined with rugged brick walls, smooth acid-washed plaster and terracotta tiles create a pleasant partnership with the landscape.

Built around the garden, pool and spa, the rear courtyard expresses an ancient motif derived from Middle Eastern precedents. Moorish influences are evident in the design of this outside space, with its gardens, fountains and pools ringed by elegant arcades and a sublime terrace. An extension of the inner courtyard, this outdoor living area comprises a mix of complementary building materials that repeat the artisanship found throughout the home. Scored concrete lined with terracotta tiles helps to define the idyllic piazza, which offers an open, sunlit sitting area adjacent to an extensive loggia. An airy arcade of cast columns and graceful arches shelters the transitional spaces of the court, easing the approach from the indoors. The pool and spa area establishes a link to the Andalusian vernacular with an animated border of geometric mosaic tile that typifies ancient Moorish motifs. Wholly integrated with the region, the rear courtyard's sense of proportion and balance offers unity to the site.

A combination of native elements, sophisticated architecture and luxe amenities, the loggia and terrace present a comfortable outdoor living zone with plenty of places to gather, dine and sunbathe. The sheltered spaces are linked to the indoors via a fluid gallery—with four sets of French doors—that unifies the private realm and culminates in a servery and wet bar easily accessed from the outside. Separate entrance to the terrace is provided via the morning room, which adjoins the kitchen's food-preparation area, and the owners' retreat, which opens to a secluded outer space.

Previous Page Left | Exposed roof trusses lend dimension and scale to the voluminous great room, a grand space which links to the courtyard through a row of French doors.

Previous Page Right | The house surrounds the central courtyard—an expansive outdoor living space with such splendid amenities as a massive hearth and an alfresco sitting area.

Above | French doors open the master bedroom to a private area of the rear property, which features a pool, spa and terraced garden.

Above Left | In the master bath, separate vanities frame a spa-style tub with a mosaic-tile surround, brightened by natural light brought in through a muntin window.

Below Left | Beamed ceilings add character to the formal dining room—an airy space that receives natural light through a series of windows, and leads to the central courtyard through the left gallery.

Above Right | At the front of the plan, the casita provides a morning bar, a full bath, a walk-in closet and French doors that lead to the side property.

Below Right | The kitchen features a soaring 19-foot ceiling that adds a sense of grandeur to the serving area. Well-crafted cabinetry sets off sleek appliances and a ceramic tile backsplash.

18543

Above | Cast-concrete forms, slurried masonry walls and a scalloped entresol create a layered façade that masterfully integrates the elevation with the ambient character of the site.

Opposite Page | A colonnade of gently sculpted arches and cast columns forms the airy perimeter of the loggia, an outside space that invites an enjoyment of nature. A formal garden influences the tailored softscapes, evocative of the terraced plant life that invigorates Iberian estates.

The Sycamores
at Shady Canyon

Rooted in the revival architecture of southern Spain, this grand *cortijo*, or hacienda-style courtyard home, presents a simple front expression to the street, with decorative Moorish-tile trim enhancing a smooth stucco finish. Varying rooflines clad in clay tiles reiterate the sculptural forms of the exterior and employ timeless themes to establish a sense of history. Designed for sidewalk-friendly neighborhoods, the elevation includes three garages—split with a swing drive and set back from the street—without allowing them to dominate the forward presence of the house. Through the side gate, an entry arcade announced by a massive, alder-plank door forecasts the grandeur of the design and offers a hint of what's to come. The passageway—sheltered by the portico above—directs guests to the formal entry and effects an easy transition from the bustle of the streetscape to the tranquility of the interior.

Design elements descended from the rural styles of Andalusia engage the flexible outer living zones with a deep level of comfort. Spaces leading in and out of the home are animated by sunlight moving through the arches, and the changing hues of the sky, trees and earth. Deep windows capture views and allow a dynamic play of shadows and light against raw mixes of masonry and wood. Decorative tile and highly sophisticated details mark the influence of Moorish dialects. Subtle schemes of tightly patterned yellow, blue and green tiles enrich sculpted archways and recessed doors and windows. Colonial architecture, defined by spare lines and dark wood trusses, is simpatico with refined embellishments derived from Andalusian themes. A sculpted masonry surround enriches the fireplace in the great room, which is framed by interior windows that permit glimpses of the stairway and wine cellar. Wainscoting elevates the design to a contemporary interpretation of Spanish Colonial style.

Interlocking spaces create highly flexible zones that facilitate the dynamics of everyday life. The grand public area invites traditional gatherings and merges with the outdoors via a series of French doors leading to a loggia and side courtyard. To the front of the plan, the library extends the spatial dimensions of the foyer, and provides a parlor-like setting for conversation or easily converts to a home office or study. With a separate approach apart from the main house, the casita offers guest quarters or an office or studio. The upper level harbors a secondary suite and space that converts to guest quarters.

BUILDER: **GREYSTONE HOMES—A LENNAR COMPANY**
LOCATION: IRVINE, CALIFORNIA

PHOTOGRAPHY: **ERIC FIGGE**

First Floor

About The Floor Plan: With a two-story presentation at the street, the house is oriented to the side courtyards. Side-gabled roofs set off a façade that achieves a significant approach from the sidewalk, with a portico that decisively establishes the place of entry. The perimeter of the home is strong and planal, with an ordered symmetry that relates to a pedestrian-friendly environment, scaled to the natural terrain. The I-shaped plan comprises two major architectural components linked by the living and dining room, which creates a boundary for opposing courtyards. An extensive gallery connects the public and private elements of the plan, and crosses the foyer to become an outdoor colonnade that leads to the casita. The design maintains a human scale with well-defined rooms and a modest circulation, yet conveys spontaneity and a sense of playfulness with open galleries, sculpted arches and access to the outdoors. Even secluded spaces at the far end of the plan permit intrusions of scenery. Panels of glass and sets of French doors open the home to outside living areas that extend the visual dimensions of the rooms and allow an interplay of light and shadows that alters the symmetry of the design. Despite a certain formality at the heart of the home, the public rooms maintain a casual, impromptu spirit that inspires a sense of comfort.

Opposite Page | Exposed trusses subdue the volume of the living room and complement a series of clerestory windows that bring in natural light. French doors open to the outside and interior windows permit glimpses of the wine room and central stairs.

Second Floor

4,820 SQUARE FEET

1 Entry	13 Pantry
2 Loggia	14 Master Bedroom
3 Entry Courtyard	15 Master Bathroom
4 Library	16 Powder Room
5 Gallery Hall	17 Bedroom
6 Living Room	18 Bathroom
7 Dining Room	19 Casita
8 Courtyard	20 Wine Room
9 Family Room	21 Laundry
10 Kitchen	22 Garage
11 Morning Room	23 Game Room
12 Butler's Pantry	24 Balcony

Previous Page | A current interpretation of the traditional courtyard plan indigenous to southern Spain and parts of Mexico, the house integrates the riches of the local terrain with timeless design elements and materials such as stucco, wrought iron and tile.

Above Left | French doors open the master bedroom to a side courtyard and capture a panorama of sky, trees and indigenous growth. The opposing wall allows access to a secluded loggia that permits fresh air and views without sacrificing the privacy of the owners.

Above Right | Adorned with paneled cabinetry and pecan-hued hardwood floors, the master bath integrates traditional accoutrements with 21st-century amenities: a spa-style tub and ceramic tile surround, and a tropical walk-through shower.

Below | An open arrangement of the family room and kitchen takes in natural light through a wall of windows and permits a vista of the morning room. Rough-hewn beams, paneled cabinetry and warm hues create an inviting place for people to gather.

Above | Just off the entry, the library offers an intimate space for conversation or a quiet area for reading. Dark timber beams establish the rugged character of the design, while subdued interior vistas reveal the home's more current disposition.

It's In The
Details

Loggia & Courtyard

The arcaded courtyard of this revival villa maintains a romantic atmosphere that is reinforced by elements derived from the Andalusian vernacular. Pure Hispanic forms are reinterpreted and applied in a more current setting. Massive square columns evoke the fortitude of colonnades lining ancient Mission-style walls, while an eclectic character permits variations on the original theme. Classic cast-concrete Doric columns border the upper portico, creating an airy, transparent outdoor space that captures breezes and remains open to views. Visually connected to the courtyard below, the balcony offers upper rooms a cooling system of cross-ventilation that is repeated on the main level. Open timber beams line the loggia roof, echoing a repetition of graceful arches along the corridor. Thick stucco walls inspired by early adobe dwellings express the primal qualities of the plan's heritage.

Since the Mediterranean climate is strikingly similar to sun-filled Southern California, this Anglo version of hacienda style takes on a diverse and interesting mix of materials and forms from regional Spanish architecture. The transitional space from the streetscene to the front door is decisively defined by the substantial columns of the entry arcade. Fieldstone pavers complement the rough-hewn timbers along the passageway, and the rustic feel of the outdoor space contradicts the highly refined painted-tile surround of the entry. Designed to provide an intermediate degree of privacy between the public sidewalk and the courtyard, the colonnade features views of the courtyard that are in harmony with the relaxed symmetry of the space.

Opposite Page | A side courtyard and loggia link secondary quarters with the master retreat and extend the visual dimensions of the living and dining room. The outside space reflects an affinity for elements true to the plan's cultural origins.

Below | A series of arches breaks the scale of the long hall leading to the family room—a space planned for views and natural light. Open to the kitchen and morning room, the casual living zone flexes to accommodate large gatherings as well as groups of two or three.

Above | The gallery hall flows uninterrupted through the entire length of the plan and all of the public rooms pivot off this axis. Mosaic tile set into the entry portal captures the warm palette of hues found throughout the home.

The Sycamores
at Shady Canyon

True to its Hispanic provenance, this courtyard villa represents a quiet integration of landscape and structure with elemental transitions to the outdoors. A 21st-century translation of Spanish Colonial and Monterey styles, the neo-vintage elevation sits unobtrusively on its site, melded with the terrain and well suited to its natural environment. Deeply sculpted recesses punctuate the weathered brick façade and heighten the impact of the forward balcony, which cantilevers above a trio of windows framing the entry. A rich dialogue of contrasting materials sets off the presentation to the street. Sienna-hued balusters, turned posts and railings enhance the authentic vocabulary of cast arches, wrought-iron sconces and buff-colored masonry. Pavers lead through the front gate and covered porch to an extensive patio, garden and terrace, providing a processional experience to the home's formal entry. Without affecting livability, the plan achieves a genuine response to the requirements of the vernacular. Transition spaces connect the interior with the outdoors, and link a progression of highly functional rooms in a rectilinear arrangement that flows from formal to informal realms. Throughout the home, the living areas correspond to inhabitable exterior spaces, creating an inner perimeter infused with a sense of nature. Sunlight from the courtyard activates the inside architecture and enlivens the interplay of rough and smooth textures. Dramatic spatial sequences heightened by the impact of high-volume places help merge indoor and outside zones. Upstairs, a gallery hall links the vaulted entry chamber with the master retreat. A series of windows offers outdoor views that expand the visual dimensions of the suite and invite an appreciation of the surrounding terrain. Two secondary bedrooms pivot off the upper chamber, engaging vistas of the courtyard and capturing sweeping views of the rolling hills and canyons.

BUILDER: **GREYSTONE HOMES—A LENNAR COMPANY**
LOCATION: IRVINE, CALIFORNIA

PHOTOGRAPHY: ERIC FIGGE

About The Floor Plan: A mosaic-tile fountain anchors the processional approach to the formal entry, sheltered by a stately turret that dominates the courtyard. Inside, the foyer surrounds an elegant spiral staircase that leads to upper-level sleeping quarters. The entry rotunda links the formal rooms to an open arrangement of the casual living spaces and the kitchen. The perimeter is lined with a series of windows that allow natural light and open vistas to oxygenate the interior. French doors open the public realm to a rear patio, which is also accessed from the morning room. The forward casita provides access to a spacious patio and outdoor fireplace—an area also linked to the library. Above the front garage, an atelier that converts to guest quarters provides a private deck with streetscene vistas.

First Floor

5,227 SQUARE FEET

1 Entry
2 Powder Room
3 Living Room
4 Dining Room
5 Courtyard
6 Kitchen
7 Nook
8 Butler's Pantry
9 Family Room
10 Home Office/Music
11 Bedroom
12 Bathroom
13 Laundry
14 Garage
15 Studio/Home Office
16 Master Bedroom
17 Master Bathroom
18 Balcony
19 Gallery Hall
20 Covered Patio

Second Floor

Previous Page Left and Right | Corbels and carved brackets outline the forward balcony, which cantilevers above a trio of windows and articulates the rich blend of Hispanic dialects. Dark wood posts and well-crafted pilasters offer eye-pleasing contrasts to pebble-hued slurried masonry, presenting a pleasing view from the street.

Opposite Page | The processional approach to the formal entry is visually enhanced by a fountain with a mosaic-tile surround. An elegant brick turret and distinctive wrought-iron balcony lend a subtle expression to the intricate detail woven into the plan.

Previous Page Left | Precast concrete forms a deeply recessed paneled entry harbored by a stately turret that dominates the courtyard. French doors create fluid boundaries with the outdoors throughout the interior.

Previous Page Right | Clerestory windows illuminate the rotunda, which opens to the living room and leads to the formal dining room via a connecting hall. A scrolled wrought-iron railing repeats the mosaic fretwork of the marble floor and the gravity-defying, soaring curves of the foyer.

Opposite page | The vaulted entry opens to a more intimate space at the foot of the stairs. Tall windows bring natural light and glimpses of scenery into the living room, which features a sculpted fireplace and hardwood floors.

Below | French doors provide access to a rear patio from the formal dining room—a thoughtful arrangement that invites lingering outside. A tall chair rail breaks the scale of the space, which is further defined by a subtle shift in color near the ceiling.

Above | A massive square arch provides a discreet perimeter for the living room, which is placed near the entry. The dramatic sequence of spaces is heightened by the volume of the foyer, which links formal and transitional spaces.

It's In The
Details

Ornamental Iron, Mosaic Tile & Sculpted Archways

A processional experience from the sidewalk through a narrow arcade to a spacious inner court culminates in the tranquility of a fountain that announces an approach to the formal entry. The mosaic-tile surround indicates elements of Moorish architecture and evokes the serenity of classic courtyard structures of southern Spain. A precast concrete sculpted archway harbors a deeply recessed entry door, framed by a refined pattern of ornamented brick. Buff-toned slurried masonry lends discreet texture to the central turret, and heightens the impact of the celebrated procession into the home. Above the paneled entry door, a well-scaled balcony features elegantly crafted and detailed wrought iron, which admirably announces the level of quality to be found throughout the home. Scrolls and filigree define the delicate minutiae of orna-

mental iron in the Spanish Revival style, and this railing sports a scalloped edge—a desirable enhancement that does not overwhelm the simple pattern of brick dentils surrounding the entry. Cast-iron sconces employ clear-glass lanterns to illuminate the space framing the paneled door. The front of the plan positions an extensive patio with a fireplace opposite the charming stairway that leads to the atelier above the forward garage. Mosaic tiles in exuberant Moorish motifs set off a traditional pattern of terracotta pavers that line the steps. Massive stucco piers echo a terraced form that lends definition and solidity to the stairway. Sleek wrought-iron railings reinforce the neo-Hispanic theme that runs throughout the exterior and inside spaces. A flattened arch adds definition to the courtyard, and transports the architecture to a new dimension.

Opposite page | Tall windows and a wrought-iron railing define the dominant gable of the rear elevation. French doors extend the livability of the formal dining room onto the terrace, which provides an alfresco sitting area.

Above | A linear arrangement of the morning room, kitchen and family room offers wide vistas and plenty of serving and food-preparation space. Bold architectural forms offer a vivid contrast to the fluid connections shared by the rooms.

Altamura
at Nellie Gail Ranch

Sited in an upscale community of fifty-two houses in Laguna Hills, the plan's distinctive Hispanic vocabulary employs a rich palette of smooth stucco, sculpted wrought iron and terra-hued clay tiles to convey the vernacular. A simple gable announces the front of the home, while a casita and recessed garage relieve the forward massing of the elevation and create a boundary for the forecourt. An ornamental tile surround enriches the entry, expresses the informality of the style and confirms a Moorish influence. Carved rafter tails articulate the authentic spirit and solidity of the plan. Overscaled to promote visibility from the street, the central turret harbors a rotunda foyer with a grand circular staircase. Sight lines extend in a number of directions from the entry: upward through the rotunda, directly ahead to the living room—with panels of scenery that capture the vistas—and toward the gallery hall, which presents an invitation for discovery of the casual living zone. Throughout the home, architectural niches, crafted Euro-style cabinetry and cast-concrete fireplace surrounds enrich the functional interior. With many adaptable amenities and floor plan options, the design allows the capacity to change over time according to the owners' preferences. The casita converts to a home office or quarters for a live-in relative. An upper-level master retreat can be transformed to an exercise room or reading space. Each of three secondary bedrooms is designed as a suite, with a private bath and a walk-in closet.

BUILDER: **WILLIAM LYON HOMES**
LOCATION: LAGUNA HILLS, CALIFORNIA

PHOTOGRAPHY: ERIC FIGGE

About The Floor Plan: A progressive approach from the sidewalk to the formal entry eases the transition to the indoors and heightens the varied presentation of the façade. The casita and forward garage define the outer perimeter of the forecourt, which offers links to the front of the home via the foyer and the morning room. The impressive plan makes a strong visual impact at the entry and introduces sight lines that terminate beyond the walls of the house.

Yet the whole plan is not apparent at the rotunda, and the informal zones are to be discovered. A gallery hall unfolds toward the family room on the ground floor and links the bonus area and secondary bedrooms on the upper level. Through the entry rotunda, the plan proceeds directly ahead through a wide archway to the living room, or up to the second floor via the grand circular staircase. Linked axially to the public realm via the butler's pantry, the kitchen is dominated by an island counter that houses dual dishwashers and sinks. Prepared for traditional events as well as impromptu family gatherings, the plan amplifies the space with architectural enhancements, such as a planning desk in the morning room and an optional wine cooler near the servery. Oriented toward rear views, the casual living zone offers access to the forecourt through French doors in the nook.

5,477 SQUARE FEET

1 Entry	9 Family Room	17 Master Bedroom
2 Courtyard	10 Nook	18 Retreat
3 Casita	11 Butler's Pantry	19 Master Bathroom
4 Living Room	12 Powder Room	20 Media Room/Game
5 Dining Room	13 Walk-In Pantry	Room
6 Gallery Hall	14 Garage	21 Bedroom
7 Wine Cellar	15 Bathroom	22 Deck
8 Kitchen	16 Library/Home Office	23 Laundry

Opposite Page | At the entry, a circular staircase brightened by clerestory windows and sight lines that extend in many directions create a strong visual impact. A mid-level landing leads to a secluded den, while a second run of curved stairs leads down to a wine cellar.

Previous Page Left | Stone pavers lead from the sidewalk to the formal entry, which is ornamented with a mosaic-tile surround and a paneled oak door. Softscapes framing the walk bear the look of the indigenous terrain.

Previous Page Right | A new look to the neighborhood draws on deep Hispanic roots, with bold, simple forms and fractured massing, intended to appear as though the house were evolved over centuries.

Second Floor

First Floor

Above | A series of windows oriented toward rear views permits natural light and scenery to brighten the family room. The space pairs an ultra-savvy multi-media center with a fireplace designed to infuse the zone with a sense of warmth and comfort.

Opposite Page | Vistas that extend beyond the living room expand the visual boundaries of the public realm. Quarry tile and open decorative beams enhance the up-to-date spirit of the home, expressed by clean lines and wide open spaces.

Benchley Hill
at Amerige Heights

In a neighborhood of tree-lined streets near one of the more established cities in Orange County, this inviting Spanish elevation displays an array of historic details: ornamental wrought-iron trim, a clay-tile roof and a sculpted, recessed entry. An arch-top window set divided by a precast column evokes the graceful tall windows of early Mediterranean houses. Simple two-story massing conveys the charm of provincial Andalusian villas, with a forecourt that promotes a street-friendly presence. An eye-pleasing continuity connects the entry court and balcony, defined by low masonry walls and cast-iron accents. A single garage is exposed to the street view and counters a side-loading, two-bay garage—a suitable arrangement that maintains the home's exceptional curb appeal. Natural light enriches the playful spirit of the home, which offers great links between the inside living areas and outdoor spaces. The formal rooms borrow scenery through a rear wall of glass that includes a trio of French doors.

Clustered informal living spaces include a morning nook that opens the casual eating area to the outdoors and activates the forecourt. In the family room, a media niche and an extended-hearth fireplace invite frequent gatherings. The gourmet kitchen offers European-style cabinetry and up-to-the-minute appliances, with wrapping food-preparation counters and separate serving areas. An optional wine cooler, a walk-in pantry and a menu-planning desk add to the livability of the informal zone. Upstairs, the bonus room—raised two steps from the central hall—is spacious enough for a game table and a media center. Secluded from the secondary bedrooms, the expansive master suite features an angled fireplace and opens to the outdoors via a rear balcony. The owners' bath includes separate vanities and a dressing area framed by two sizeable walk-in closets. An exercise area receives sunlight through the forward windows and leads to the front balcony by way of French doors.

BUILDER: **PARDEE HOMES**
LOCATION: FULLERTON, CALIFORNIA

PHOTOGRAPHY: **ROBB MILLER**
RENDERING: **RAY HART**

3,473 SQUARE FEET

1 Entry Courtyard	8 Kitchen	15 Master Bedroom
2 Entry	9 Nook	16 Master Bathroom
3 Gallery Hall	10 Walk-in Pantry	17 Exercise Room
4 Living Room	11 Bedroom	18 Deck
5 Dining Room	12 Bathroom	19 Garage
6 Powder Room	13 Laundry	
7 Family Room	14 Bonus Room	

Second Floor

First Floor

About The Floor Plan: This Andalusian-inspired elevation features a split three-car garage with a swing drive that helps diminish the garage presence at the streetscape. A deeply recessed entry and rows of square and arch-top windows achieve a captivating rhythm of fenestration derived from early Mediterranean dialects. A detailed wrought-iron gate leads to an intimate entry court framed by the forward gables, creating a processional experience to the front door, central foyer and staircase. The two-story elevation harbors a disciplined footprint of generous and balanced spaces bounded only by views and glimpses of scenery. With well-defined rooms and links to the outdoors, the home boasts a highly efficient circulation. A floor plan derived from centuries-old hacienda styles stays true to authentic compositions, which permit seamless boundaries between rooms and outside spaces. A horizontal spine connects the plan on both levels, fostering the flow between formal and casual areas. The kitchen is organized as the informal hub of the home, with a built-in planning desk and plenty of seating around the center island and along the snack bar. Upstairs, a vertical axis aligns the sumptuous spaces of the master retreat. At its terminus, an exercise room with a private deck offers convenience as well as repose for the owners.

Below | Sage-green walls lend an air of serenity to the master bath and soften the contrasts between cloud-white fixtures and slate-gray floors. Separate vanities frame a floating spa-style tub with a surround made of natural stone.

Above | A central food-preparation island anchors the open kitchen and offers seating for family gatherings— an arrangement that reflects the new function of the kitchen as the central activity hub in today's home.

Above | Rough-hewn timber posts, wrought-iron balusters and twin arched windows express the true Spanish origins of this street-friendly home. The forecourt provides a progressive experience from the sidewalk through the courtyard to the formal entry.

Stone Canyon Preserve

Bordered by a wilderness park and a stone's throw from the historic Padua Hills Theatre, this community overlooks a series of canyons and riparian basins in the foothills of the San Gabriel Mountains. Located in Claremont, the homes establish an historic ambience with hybrid versions of classic Spanish Colonial Revival and Santa Barbara styles. Residence Two captures the spirit of southern Spain with an Andalusian-inspired courtyard design, which harbors a spacious outdoor living area and a loggia with an alfresco fireplace. Single-story elements capped with barrel-tile roofs surround the structure, interposed with a taller gable that faces the street and a two-story wing that includes a fourth bedroom and bonus space. Paneled garage doors enrich the forward presentation without dominating the façade, and a shed roof tops a side-loading single-car garage. Inside, a wrapping gallery integrates a series of rooms with independent links to the outside—through windows, bays and French doors.

BUILDER: **CENTEX HOMES**
LOCATION: CLAREMONT, CALIFORNIA

PHOTOGRAPHY: ERIC FIGGE

Opposite Page | Simple white elements set off the fractured and layered composition, adorned with decorative tile and punctuated by recessed windows and wrought-iron grillwork.

Below | Terracotta-paver floors unify the courtyard with the loggia, which provides an outdoor fireplace and an interior view to the family room.

Above | The graceful arch of a parabolic window elevates a Moorish motif to sheer glamour in the living room—a light-infused space with a link to the courtyard.

Stone Canyon Preserve

Near the historic town of Claremont, California, and neighbor to the Angeles National Forest, Stone Canyon Preserve integrates rustic and refined elements in eco-conscious designs that reflect their natural surroundings. Residence Four offers a pleasing approach from the sidewalk, with relatively simple massing punctuated with tall windows and deep recesses that express its Spanish origins. A tandem garage works with a side-loading counterpart—also with a two-car capacity—to enhance the street presentation and maintain the human scale of the elevation. Hip rooflines reduce the vertical scale of the Spanish Colonial Revival façade, enlivened by rolled-up stucco eaves that lend a clean horizontal finish. Neoclassical cast-concrete elements understate the entry and repeat the rectilinear forms of the elevation. Flexible rooms throughout the plan offer myriad options to the owners, allowing customization of each residence.

BUILDER: **CENTEX HOMES**
LOCATION: CLAREMONT, CALIFORNIA

PHOTOGRAPHY: ERIC FIGGE

Opposite Page | Canvas awnings held up with iron stanchions express Andalusian beginnings. A forward balcony supported by a simple Doric column and attached with a sculpted lazy-arch wall offers a surprise at the front elevation.

Above Right | An open gallery hall extends sight lines to the formal dining room and softens the high-volume vertical scale of the living room.

Below Right | An optional guest suite developed to include a separate sitting space opens to the central courtyard through French doors.

CHAPTER THREE

ON-THE-BOARD PROJECTS

Sheshan Golf Resort
Shanghai, China

J ust north of Sheshan Mountain, in the heart of Shanghai's National Resort Park, this 15,000-acre community features a postcard-perfect landscape dotted with cypress and bamboo groves, olive trees and vineyards. Hosts of 2,000-year-old ginkgo trees surround this remarkable community—located just forty kilometers east of Shanghai's metro center—where indigenous wetlands are crisscrossed with picturesque walkways and foot bridges. A winding path leads up to the crest of the mountain where Sheshan Cathedral— a neo-Romanesque structure built by the French Catholic Church in the 1930s—overlooks the resort's waterways and private residences. Visually integrated with the native terrain, the townhomes and detached luxury villas of this unique development surround three common structures: the Golf Clubhouse, Community Center and Beach Club. Located near the former site of a clay quarry, the project creates a refined landscape of fairways and watercourses, including a system of cascading rapids interspersed with jagged rocks harvested from the mine.

Lush softscapes enrich a grouping of 120 luxury villas, which feature French and Tuscan elevations and a selection of five distinct interior plans. Designed with stone, barrel-tile roofs and weathered stucco, the rustic, manor-house elevations evoke the humble character of rural Mediterranean styles. Handcrafted hardwood and ceramic-tile floors complement scrolled wrought-iron fixtures and earthen-hued furnishings throughout the interiors, creating a textured, contemporary décor with bold links to the past.

The homeowner's private retreat includes a study that reflects a deep appreciation of Chinese culture, while the master bedroom features elegant splashes of vibrant color and vistas of scenery. Open kitchens boast up-to-the-minute appliances and lead to morning nooks and formal dining rooms with wide views of the golf course. Each design also features a multi-functional basement with plenty of natural light, a home theater or media center, and an exercise room. Guest quarters and kids' rooms are designed with varied palettes that permit views and links to nature, and every villa enjoys a private garden and a wide veranda. The attached townhomes also feature individual gardens and terraces.

BUILDER: **UNIFRONT ENTERPRISE INVESTMENT CO., LTD.**

ILLUSTRATIONS: **MILO OLEA**
SITE PLAN GRAPHIC: **AARON MARTINEZ**

Golf Clubhouse

Community Center

Villas

Beach Club

Townhomes

About The Site Plan: At the entry gate, a massive arch announces the Tuscan style of the project, with wide views of surging manmade rapids to the left of the main drive. Surrounded by water in three directions, the project integrates its public spaces with pristine fairways, quaint bridges, footpaths and places to meditate. A primary watercourse, lined with trees on both banks, separates a neighborhood of 120 luxury villas from clusters of townhomes, which are grouped into two-, three- and five-plexes. Yue Lake enhances the view from the villas and creates a natural boundary between the development and the hustle and bustle of the outside world.

A trio of public structures shares common space at the heart of the project. To the front of this area, the Community Center provides a porte cochere that connects the entry drive to a foyer leading to shops, restaurants, cafes and pubs.

To the right of the hall, business offices flank a conference center that allows wide vistas of the lake. The Golf Clubhouse situated on a sloping site extends a colonnade and porte cochere to the street, permitting guests to enter the foyer on the upper floor. Inside, panoramas of the fairway illuminate the main hall, which offers access to a gracefully curved terrace with a fireplace, and features a restaurant and bar, a host of VIP rooms and a pro shop that leads directly down to the first tee. A third level provides 120-degree views of the golf course, while a walkout basement includes separate lounges and dressing spaces for men and women, saunas and vanities, private showers and three pools. The Beach Club features a health club with a natatorium and spa. Rows of cherrywood lockers, a meditation room, and an exercise studio for aerobics, weight-lifting and dance classes, complement a full menu of shops and services.

Opposite Page | Clusters of luxury villas share panoramas of Yue Lake and glimpses of the fairway. The common areas help to define the property and create a link to a community of clustered residences.

Above | The Golf Clubhouse offers a true sense of the rural Tuscan environment, with a rugged elevation that overlooks a rustic footbridge and waterway.

Above | At the terminus of a scenic entry drive, the
Community Center offers an inviting street presentation
of varied rooflines and gables, and provides access to an
array of shops, pubs and restaurants.

Artist's concept only - final project may differ.

Rear Elevation

Castellina
The Covenant at Ladera Ranch

Located in the picturesque community of Covenant Hills at Ladera Ranch, Castellina is a new neighborhood slated for eighty-two single- and two-story attached villas designed to capture the spirit of a Tuscan hilltown. Walkable streets and quiet cul-de-sacs track the contours of the gently sloping terrain throughout the village, interposed with random scenic overlooks, pedestrian-friendly parks and piazza-style turnabouts. Lush arcadian softscapes tuned to the topography and climate of Tuscany reinforce the quaint rural ambience of the neighborhood's integrated design. Animated elevations and varied exterior forms in earthen textures and hues will lend a sense of informality to the development, unified by recurring elements, such as interlocking pavers and intricately crafted architectural details. Just nine miles from the Pacific Ocean, the project will feature attached plans that are integrated to the sites by cultivated landscapes and refined mixes of natural materials: stone, wood and iron details that enrich the articulated exterior finishes. Oriented toward scenic views throughout the property, the homes will present strong aesthetics on all four sides of each building. Structural massing using loggias and upper-level verandas will vary and create intriguing visual connections with the common areas, promoting a sense of the hilltown experience. French doors and rows of tall windows line the perimeters of the plans, dissolving the definitions of indoors and out with expansive views of scenery. The careful arrangement of flexible rooms and wide open spaces is designed to appeal to the move-down buyer.

BUILDER: **CENTEX HOMES**
LOCATION: LADERA RANCH, CALIFORNIA

RENDERINGS: **RAY HART**

Second Floor

First Floor

Artist's concept only - final project may differ.

Front Elevation

Basement Level

Crystal Cove
at Newport Coast

Just above the classic beach village of Crystal Cove—a state-protected area that includes an idyllic stretch of beach and enviable vistas—this singular collection of homes makes an unprecedented statement about style and livability. Influenced by a broad mix of Mediterranean dialects, this primarily Tuscan design offers a central sunken courtyard, with an entry, forecourt and foyer to the front of the plan. The highly refined street presentation reveals an advanced architecture that enhances the function and character of the home, and evolves to a deeply comfortable plan. An enfilade of rooms progresses from a casita and guest suite to the casual living area, positioned to the left of the master suite. The formal dining room adjoins a vertical gallery leading to a secluded home office.

BUILDER: **STANDARD PACIFIC HOMES**

First Floor
(Second floor not shown)

Front Elevation

Rear Elevation

Section

Section

Artist's concept only - final project may differ.

Annotated Projects List

Altamura
Residence Two
Laguna Hills, California
2003
Pages 128-133

Bassenian/Lagoni Architects Team:
Designers: Dave Pockett,
  Mike Pilarski
Project Managers: Sophia Braverman,
  John Oravetz

Builder: William Lyon Homes
Builder Executive in Charge of Design:
  Tom Mitchell
Landscape Architect: Urban Arena
Interior Designer: Design Tec Interiors
Structural Engineer: Performance Plus
  Engineering

Photographer: Eric Figge

Benchley Hill
Residence Two
Fullerton, California
2002 – 2003
Pages 134-137

Bassenian/Lagoni Architects Team:
Designers: John Bigot AIA,
  Jennifer Cram
Project Managers: Roberta Jeannette,
  Bryce Hove

Builder: Pardee Homes
Builder Executive in Charge of Design:
  Bob Clauser
Landscape Architect: SJA
Interior Designer: Color Design Art
Structural Engineer: Borm Associates

Photographer: Robb Miller

Rendering: Ray Hart

Awards:
Gold Nuggets 2003
  Merit Award
MAME/Southern California 2003
  Finalists
    Residence Two
    Best Detached Community

Canyon's Edge
Residence Three
Irvine, California
2003
Pages 40-45

Bassenian/Lagoni Architects Team:
Designers: Dave Kosco AIA,
  Hans Anderle
Project Managers: Gerry Esser,
  Javier Gomez

Builder: Standard Pacific – Gallery
  Communities
Builder Executive in Charge of Design:
  Ralph Spargo
Landscape Architect: Summers/Murphy
  & Partners
Interior Designer: Saddleback Interiors
Structural Engineer: Structures Design
  Group

Photographer: Lance Gordon

Graphics: Aaron Martinez

Awards:
Best in American Living Awards 2003
  Platinum Winner
Gold Nuggets 2004
  Merit Award

**The Cortile Collection
at The Bridges**
Residence One
Rancho Santa Fe, California
2003 – 2004
Pages 14-25

Bassenian/Lagoni Architects Team:
Designers: Dave Kosco AIA,
  Craig Gambill AIA
Project Managers: Brian Neves AIA,
  Mike Beam, Jeff Ganyo

Builder: HCC Investors/Lennar
  Communities
Builder Executive in Charge of Design:
  Tom Martin
Landscape Architect: Pinnacle Design
Interior Designer: Pacific Dimensions
Structural Engineer: Performance Plus
  Engineering

Photographer: Eric Figge

Awards:
Gold Nuggets 2004
  Merit Award
  Grand Award – Detached Residential
    Community of the Year
SAM 2004 Finalist

**The Cortile Collection
at The Bridges**
Residence Two
Rancho Santa Fe, California
2003 – 2004
Pages 92-105

Bassenian/Lagoni Architects Team:
Designers: Dave Kosco AIA,
Craig Gambill AIA
Project Managers: Brian Neves AIA,
Mike Beam, Jeff Ganyo

Builder: HCC Investors/Lennar
Communities
Builder Executive in Charge of Design:
Tom Martin
Landscape Architect: Pinnacle Design
Interior Designer: Pacific Dimensions
Structural Engineer: Performance Plus
Engineering

Photographer: Eric Figge

Awards:
Best in American Living Awards 2004
Platinum Award
The Nationals 2004
Silver Award
Gold Nuggets 2004
Grand Awards
Residence Two
Detached Residential Community
of the Year
SAM 2004 Finalist

**The Cortile Collection
at The Bridges**
Residence Three
Rancho Santa Fe, California
2003 – 2004
Pages 26-39

Bassenian/Lagoni Architects Team:
Designers: Dave Kosco AIA,
Craig Gambill AIA
Project Managers: Brian Neves AIA,
Mike Beam, Jeff Ganyo

Builder: HCC Investors/Lennar
Communities
Builder Executive in Charge of Design:
Tom Martin
Landscape Architect: Pinnacle Design
Interior Designer: Pacific Dimensions
Structural Engineer: Performance Plus
Engineering

Photographer: Eric Figge

Awards:
Builder's Choice Awards 2004
Grand Award
Best in American Living Awards 2004
Platinum Award & Best in Region
The Nationals 2004
Gold Award & Best in Region
Gold Nuggets 2004
Grand Awards
Residence Three
Home of the Year
Detached Residential Community
of the Year
MAME/Southern California 2003 – Winner
SAM 2004 Finalist

Cover:
Professional Builder, January 2004

**DeFelice Residence
at Shady Canyon**
Irvine, California
2004
Pages 46-55

Bassenian/Lagoni Architects Team:
Designers: Kevin Karami,
Hans Anderle
Project Managers: Gerry Esser,
Javier Gomez

Client: Ron & Vicky DeFelice
Builder: Warmington Custom Homes
Builder Executives in Charge of Design:
Larry Riggs, Matt White
Structural Engineer: Gouvis Engineering

Photographer: Eric Figge

Awards:
The Nationals 2004
Gold Award & Best in Region

Shady Canyon Residence
Irvine, California
2004
Pages 56-61

Bassenian/Lagoni Architects Team:
Designer: Kevin Karami
Project Managers: Gerry Esser,
Javier Gomez

Builder: Warmington Custom Homes
Builder Executives in Charge of Design:
Larry Riggs, Matt White
Structural Engineer: Gouvis Engineering

Photographer: Eric Figge

Stone Canyon Preserve
Residence Two
Claremont, California
2004
Pages 138-139

Bassenian/Lagoni Architects Team:
Designers: Kevin Karami,
John Bigot AIA
Project Managers: Brian Cameron,
Eric Widmer

Builder: Centex Homes – LA/Ventura
Division
Builder Executive in Charge of Design:
Mark Kohler
Landscape Architect: LA Group
Interior Designer: Creative Design
Consultants
Structural Engineer: Performance Plus
Engineering

Photographer: Eric Figge

Awards:
The Nationals 2004
Detached Community of the Year
Elan 2004
Finalist
Residence Two
Winner
Project of the Year

Stone Canyon Preserve
Residence Four
Claremont, California
2004
Pages 140-141

Bassenian/Lagoni Architects Team:
Designers: Kevin Karami,
John Bigot AIA
Project Managers: Brian Cameron,
Eric Widmer

Builder: Centex Homes – LA/Ventura
Division
Builder Executive in Charge of Design:
Mark Kohler
Landscape Architect: LA Group
Interior Designer: Creative Design
Consultants
Structural Engineer: Performance Plus
Engineering

Photographer: Eric Figge

Awards:
The Nationals 2004
Residence Four - Silver Award
Detached Community of the Year
Elan 2004
Winners
Residence Four
Project of the Year

The Sycamores at Shady Canyon
Residence One
Irvine, California
2004
Pages 82-91

Bassenian/Lagoni Architects Team:
Designers: Kevin Karami,
Albern Yolo
Project Managers: Jeff Marcotte,
Ryan Rosecrans

Builder: Greystone Homes – A Lennar
Company
Builder Executives in Charge of Design:
Tom Martin, Doug Woodward
Landscape Architect: HRP LanDesign
Interior Designer: Trio Design Group
Structural Engineer: Dale Christian

Photographer: Eric Figge

Awards:
Gold Nuggets 2004
Merit Awards
Residence One
Detached Community of the Year
MAME/Southern California 2003
Finalist
Detached Community Award

The Sycamores at Shady Canyon
Residence Two
Irvine, California
2004
Pages 106-115

Bassenian/Lagoni Architects Team:
Designers: Kevin Karami,
Albern Yolo
Project Managers: Jeff Marcotte,
Ryan Rosecrans

Builder: Greystone Homes – A Lennar
Company
Builder Executives in Charge of Design:
Tom Martin, Doug Woodward
Landscape Architect: HRP LanDesign
Interior Designer: Trio Design Group
Structural Engineer: Dale Christian

Photographer: Eric Figge

Awards:
Gold Nuggets 2004
Merit Awards
Residence Two
Detached Community of the Year
MAME/Southern California 2003
Finalists
Residence Two
Detached Community Award

Cover:
Builder Magazine, September 2004

On-The-Boards

Castellina at Ladera Ranch
Ladera Ranch, California
2005
Pages 150-151

Bassenian/Lagoni Architects Team:
Designers: Dave Kosco AIA,
Kevin Karami
Project Managers: Jeff Ganyo,
Ian Sparks, Maleck Elahi

Builder: Centex Homes – South Coast
Division
Builder Executive in Charge of Design:
Nick Lehnert

Renderings: Ray Hart

The Sycamores at Shady Canyon
Residence Three
Irvine, California
2004
Pages 116-127

Bassenian/Lagoni Architects Team:
Designers: Kevin Karami,
Albern Yolo
Project Managers: Jeff Marcotte,
Ryan Rosecrans

Builder: Greystone Homes – A Lennar
Company
Builder Executives in Charge of Design:
Tom Martin, Doug Woodward
Landscape Architect: HRP LanDesign
Interior Designer: Trio Design Group
Structural Engineer: Dale Christian

Photographer: Eric Figge

Awards:
Best in American Living Awards 2004
Gold Award
Builder's Choice Awards 2004
Merit Award
Gold Nuggets 2004
Merit Awards
Residence Three
Detached Community of the Year
MAME/Southern California 2003
Finalists
Residence Three
Detached Community Award

Ultimate Family Home
Las Vegas, Nevada
2003
Pages 70-81

Bassenian/Lagoni Architects Team:
Designers: Jeff Lake AIA,
Dave Kosco AIA, Kevin Karami
Project Manager: Ken Niemerski AIA

Client: Builder Magazine
Builder: Pardee Homes
Builder Executive in Charge of Design:
Bob Clauser
Landscape Architect: Lifescapes
International
Interior Designer: Color Design Art
Structural Engineer: Borm Associates

Photographer: Eric Figge

Awards:
Gold Nuggets 2004
Merit Award

Covers:
Builder Magazine, January 2004
HOME Magazine, February 2004

Villa Firenze
Renaissance at Stonetree Golf Club
Novato, California
2002
Pages 66-67

Bassenian/Lagoni Architects Team:
Designers: Kevin Karami,
John Bigot AIA
Project Managers: Sophia Braverman,
Dwayne Butz

Builder: Davidon Homes
Builder Executive in Charge of Design:
Don Chaiken
Landscape Architect: Rose Associates
Interior Designer: Creative Design
Consultants
Structural Engineer: Gouvis Engineering

Photographer: Tim Maloney
Image supplied by Trends Publishing
USA, Inc.

Whispering Glen
Irvine, California
2003
Pages 62-65

Bassenian/Lagoni Architects Team:
Designers: Kevin Karami,
Albern Yolo
Project Managers: Marty Lopez,
Nate Rodholm

Builder: Shea Homes
Builder Executive in Charge of Design:
Les Thomas
Landscape Architect: Forma
Interior Designer: Pacific Dimensions
Structural Engineer: ESI/FME Engineering

Photographer: Will Hare, Jr.

Awards:
Gold Nuggets 2004
Merit Award
Best Attached Project
Gold Nuggets 2003
Merit Awards
Best Attached Project
Best Attached Project of the Year

Sheshan Golf Club
Pudong, Shanghai, China
2003-2004
Pages 144-149

Bassenian/Lagoni Architects Team:
Designers: Ray Hart – Villas, Community
Center and Beach Club
Craig Gambill AIA – Golf Clubhouse
Ernie Gorrill AIA – Townhomes

Builder: Unifront Enterprise Investment
Co., Ltd.
Builder Executive in Charge of Design:
Xiaohong Dan

Crystal Cove
Newport Beach, California
2004
Pages 152-153

Bassenian/Lagoni Architects Team:
Designers: Kevin Karami,
Dave Kosco AIA, Joe Abrajano

Builder: Standard Pacific Homes –
Gallery Communities
Builder Executive in Charge of Design:
Ralph Spargo

Staff List 2004

Executive Staff
Aram Bassenian
Carl Lagoni
Scott Adams
Steven Dewan
Kevin Karami
Dave Kosco
Jeff LaFetra
Jeff Lake
Ken Niemerski
Lee Rogaliner

Vice Presidents
Ali Badie
Mike Beam
Brian Neves
Dave Pockett

Associate Vice President
Ernie Gorrill

Director, China Region
Yao Wang

Senior Associates
Hans Anderle
Craig Gambill
Jeff Marcotte

Associates
Sophia Braverman
Dave Day
Judy Forrester
Jeff Ganyo
Ray Hart
Marty Lopez
Edie Motoyama
Wendy Woolsey

General Staff
Joe Abrajano
Raffi Agaian
Stacie Arrigo
John Bigot
Randy Brown
Scott Bunney
Kevin Burt
Dwayne Butz
Brian Cameron
Lenz Casilan
Luis Chavez
Ellen Chen
Sue Dewan
Jenni Dillon
Kele Dooley
Dee Drylie
Maleck Elahi
Gerry Encarnacion
Elmer Evangelista
Clois Fitch
Will Francisco
Paul Fulbright
Javier Gomez
Jeff Hackett
George Handy
Elian Hernandez
Young Hong
Roberta Jeannette
Katie Kaford
Huy Le
Phillip Lee
Felix Lo
Constanza Marcheselli
Kristina McVeigh
Shawn Melendez
Tom Mkhitarian
Lauren Moss
Christina Nagel

Chris Ngo
Jo Ann O'Neill
Curtis Ong
John Oravetz
Debby Owens
Margo Penick
Mike Pilarski
Susan Pistacchi
Bob Platt
Lisa Platt
Greg Purvis
Yvonne Ramos
Mary Ring
Nate Rodholm
Ryan Rosecrans
Charlie Sawyer
Jeffry Sinarjo
Marshall Smith
Ian Sparks
Melissa Spence
Dawn Stanton
Kevin Stracner
Ryan Sullivan
Courtney Tran
Linda Vancil
Chris Velasquez
Tony Vinh
Warren Walker
Jacob Wen
Ryan White
Stacy White
Eric Widmer
John Wilmert
Michael Wu
Jason Yaw
Nick Yolla
Alex Yuan
Bernard Yuen

Index

HOMES & COURTYARDS

28 Beautifully Designed Homes For Outdoor Living

HOMES & COURTYARDS

28 Beautifully Designed Homes For Outdoor Living

BASSENIAN / LAGONI ARCHITECTS

Library of Congress Control Number:
2007924321

International Standard Book Number:
978-0-9721539-3-5 (hardcover)
0-9721539-3-4 (hardcover)

Published by Bassenian/Lagoni Architects
2031 Orchard Drive, Suite 100
Newport Beach, CA 92660-0753
Phone: 949-553-9100
Fax: 949-553-0548
www.bassenianlagoni.com

Corporate
Chairman & CEO: Aram Bassenian, AIA
President: Carl Lagoni, AIA
Executive Vice President: Jeffrey LaFetra, AIA
Chief Financial Officer: Lee Rogaliner
Senior Principals: Scott Adams, AICP
                  David Kosco, AIA
                  Jeff Lake, AIA
Principals: Ali Badie, AIA
            Steven Dewan, AIA
            Kevin Karami
            Ken Niemerski, AIA

Book Production
Editorial Director: Aram Bassenian, AIA
Editor-in-Chief: Rickard Bailey, Bailey Consulting, Inc.
Editor: Heather McCune
Writer: Laura Hurst Brown, Rascal Words, Ltd.
Design/Art Director: Edie Motoyama
Art Director/Designer, Cover Design: Zareh Marzbetuny, ZM Design
Floor Plan Graphics: Stacie Arrigo, Jennifer Cram, Edie Motoyama
Assistants to the Editorial Director: Kele Dooley, Debby Owens

Prepress by Toppan Hong Kong

Printed in China by Toppan Printing

10 9 8 7 6 5 4 3 2 1

Contents

Acknowledgements

BY ARAM BASSENIAN, AIA

Publishing has taken us on a rapid and eventful journey. It has been only two years since the publication of our second book, *Tuscan and Andalusian Reflections*, and just four years since we published our first volume, *Pure California*. Now, in *Homes and Courtyards*, we present our most extensive architectural work to date, with many of the homes emphasizing outdoor living. Such design evolution is our response to the changing needs of a robust economy in the United States and in emerging economies worldwide. There seems to be a clear recognition that home ownership is a substantial economic pillar in any growing society. To this we attribute a part of our success and for this we are thankful.

At Bassenian/Lagoni Architects, we cultivate a problem-solving and practical design attitude. Our company culture dictates that constraints are mere opportunities to be exploited for new and dynamic architecture. We firmly believe that our role is to assist the development team; thus, to us, excellence in service is a daily mantra. Therefore, we express our deep appreciation to a very unique team of talented professionals who constitute our firm. It is only the very passionate and mature design professional who has the ability to step up, time and time again, to offer fresh and diverse solutions— and we salute those in our office who do just that on a daily basis.

We are indebted as well to many of our clients, both builder and marketing executives, whose vision begins the design process for these beautiful homes and communities. They are courageous "place-makers" in the full sense of the definition. And our gratitude extends to their project managers and construction teams who embrace this vision and, through commitment and hard work, complete the mission with excellence.

We also extend sincere appreciation to our allied professionals—the structural engineers, landscape architects and interior designers who help make every new home an unfolding chapter in the American dream. It is only through total commitment to their craft that sticks and stones turn to comfort and elegance.

Lastly and importantly, I am forever indebted to my enlightened parents who willingly, and at a late age, sacrificed all to bring their children to this "shining city on the hill." Along the way they demonstrated the virtues of work, yet taught me moderation and balance in all matters of life. I am so grateful to America for affording me and my family education and, therefore, endless opportunity. And, closest to home, my deepest appreciation goes to my family for giving my life true purpose, guidance and stability.

Foreword

*This is what I prayed for ... a piece of land — not so very big,
with a garden and, near the house, a spring that never fails,
and a bit of wood to round it off.*

— Horace

Now, more than 20 centuries later, we live at a pace Horace could not have imagined in 30 B.C. In our 24/7 world, with more gadgets, Google Earth, ways to design a car or plan a vacation on-line, we multi-task to manage work, family, pets, aging parents, what to eat for dinner, and, of course, e-mail. But much like Horace, we dream about a home, *our* home on our land, a place of beauty, respite, warmth, at one with nature, a place that's right for us.

Bassenian/Lagoni Architects' magic is in creating right places. Their homes give us refuge from the hectic world and shelter in its deepest, best meaning. They ground us in the land, the courtyard gardens, the beautiful interior spaces and the diverse exteriors that enrich the neighborhoods where they are built.

Frederic March, in his book, *Thunder at Twilight*, noted that all great places have two things in common: one foot in memory and one foot in prophecy. Bassenian/Lagoni imbues their architecture with that truth — creating homes that embody the best traditions of design — through materials, proportions and architectural styles. At the same time, their work embraces and celebrates the future with clean lines, simple elegance and artful form, bringing the art in architecture to every home.

In traveling the globe, from Tuscan Italy to Moorish Spain, and from the New England coast to the American Southwest, Bassenian/Lagoni designers have tapped into the world-influences on great architecture. And they've drawn on the best of America's rich residential heritage. From Neff to Maybeck and from Gill to Wright, their work weaves together memory and prophecy.

The noted mid-century California architect, Cliff May, once designed a two-room house with a five-room garden. The courtyard homes displayed in this volume honor the notion of that connectivity. Natural light seems to penetrate each of these homes so seamlessly. Whether it is an expansive veranda or a central courtyard, the outdoors consistently activates the core and elements of each of these houses with inventiveness. Outdoor living truly has an allure all of its own and these wondrous homes blend the dreams of the owner and architect with the land and garden. Bassenian/Lagoni's work accentuates that combination in its creative best—*right places*.

As a child, I grew up on Prospect Boulevard in Pasadena — one of the streets mentioned in Allan Jacobs' *Great Streets* classic. From the camphor-tree canopy to the Wallace Neff, Greene and Greene, and Frank Lloyd Wright homes, my neighborhood was filled with architectural gems and landscape grandeur. As a youngster, I took it for granted that all neighborhoods were this wonderful. It spoiled me for the future — and made other right places so much more valuable when I found them.

In the pages of this book, you'll see homes that are distinctive and that resonate with the feeling of *right place* for the right homeowner. Therein lies the practical genius of Bassenian/Lagoni Architects' work. Whether designing a one-family custom home, like the Wine Country Residence in Paso Robles, or a whole development neighborhood, like Bella Fioré in Lake Las Vegas, Bassenian/Lagoni Architects create homes as different and distinctive as their owners, things of beauty with extraordinary character and appeal...*right places*. And like the great neighborhoods of the past, I long to live in one. That's their magic.

Introduction

TRADITION AND INNOVATION

BY ARAM BASSENIAN, AIA & CARL LAGONI, AIA

Tradition and innovation – two seemingly contradictory influences – often contribute equally to the architecture that shapes our lives. Consider the following definitions:

Tradition: an inherited, established customary pattern of thought, action or behavior; the handing down of information, beliefs, and customs from one generation to another without written instruction.

Innovation: the introduction of something new; to effect a change in something.

Architecture consistently draws inspiration from the past and modifies the original to express a new aesthetic that reflects current ways of thinking. Historical influences for our work have come from masters such as:

Andrea Palladio, one of the most influential architects in the Western world, was prolific in Northern Italy during the sixteenth century. Drawing great inspiration from classical architecture, he generated a carefully proportioned vocabulary that became the model for stately homes and government buildings in both Europe and in America.

Wallace Neff was instrumental in his impact on Southern California's early residential architecture. Reflecting the Moorish idioms of the Mediterranean climate zone, his homes designed for movie moguls appeared in the 1930s. Today, they are the epitome of that era with an eloquence untainted by the passage of time.

To architect *Charles Moore* we credit the ignition of the more playful Post-Modern movement. The significance of his contribution is immeasurable. Through him, in part, modernism was rapidly transformed, allowing architects freedom for open experimentation.

Ricardo Legorreta, a noted designer from Mexico, has authored an architectural language that combines bold, clean, colorful forms with the character of the Southwest. His work stands out for its simplicity and sculptural singularity.

These masters create designs so substantive that they seem to transcend time and place. As architects who follow, our role is to understand the essence of their work and, using today's technology and building materials, create up-to-date homes reflective of contemporary lifestyle.

Today, as a firm, we find ourselves practicing during a unique time in history. Buoyed by an expanding economy, we have multiple opportunities for creativity. At the same time, our design efforts are occurring in a highly competitive marketplace. This milieu fuels advancement and evolution — motivating us to continuously reach for the next and more sophisticated home. And through our involvement with development housing, we are gratified to touch so many in America as they pursue their home-ownership dream.

In the following pages we unveil homes that represent our current contribution to the evolving art form that is housing. With ordered architecture, fractured massing and brick and stone detailing, we recall the hill towns of Tuscany at *Castellina*. The interiors of these upscale townhomes are designed to naturally flow out to balconies, loggias and extended patios to enthusiastically connect with the soft climate of coastal Southern California.

At the *Shady Canyon Residence*, a layering of spaces is unveiled through controlled openings. A progression unfolds to reveal the spatial experiences of this unique home. Formal and informal as well as indoor and outdoor living areas are contained with unity in a rural Mediterranean theme.

The *Wine Country Residence* in Paso Robles rests on a spectacular hilltop. Combine this great site with the ideal client and you have the once-in-a-lifetime opportunity for any architectural firm. Here with crisp, contemporary lines and inspiration from Legorreta, the front and back of this dwelling open to meet the vineyards of central California.

And it all comes together at *The Tides* in Newport Coast. Residential architecture, with inspiration from Tuscany, turns to express a new aesthetic in upscale coastal living. An entry forecourt, followed by a three-story interior courtyard, is enhanced by exquisite brick and stone detailing, bringing the outdoors inside and stimulating our senses.

As you experience this photographic home tour with its attendant narrative, we hope you find in our homes and communities a respect for tradition with a flare that speaks of innovation.

CHAPTER ONE

HOMES & COURTYARDS

The Tides

BUILDER: STANDARD PACIFIC HOMES • LOCATION: NEWPORT COAST, CALIFORNIA • PHOTOGRAPHY: ANTHONY GOMEZ

R E S I D E N C E   O N E

Perched above a breathtaking stretch of the Pacific coastline, this richly detailed Mediterranean home captures the strong lines of a classic Tuscan farmhouse. Just beyond the formal entry forecourt, the house reveals its dramatic surprise: a stunning three-story second courtyard that allows sunlight and coastal breezes to penetrate and infuse the center of this magnificent home. As the sequence of spaces unfolds, the building takes shape with well-delineated mixes of stone and stucco that visually connect the house with the coastal grandeur of the site. Vistas extend beyond the rear loggia and terrace to the horizon, where glimpses of the sea confer a sense of tranquility on the home. Public rooms on the main and lower levels relate closely to the subterranean garden, a refreshing counterpoint to the rustic sophistication of the interior. Open to the sky, the courtyards complement exposure to the outdoors at the front and rear of the home, and lend light and protection from the elements at its core.

Right | Worthy of its upscale location, the house achieves visual continuity with the site and opens to an uninterrupted vista that extends from the sidewalk to the sea. Despite its apparent size and grandeur, the home contains an elegant floor plan that lives principally on one level.

Below | Centuries collide at the rear perimeter, where detailed brick surrounds, stone cladding and a trio of arches play against the clean lines of a very up-to-date home. A ribbon of vertical windows flanking the upper loggia captures vast views of the sea.

Upper Level

Subterranean Level

Legend

1 Breezeway	10 Kitchen	19 Wine Tasting Room
2 Forecourt	11 Nook	20 Home Theater
3 Foyer	12 Family Room	21 Fitness Room
4 Central Courtyard	13 Master Bedroom	22 Artist Loft
5 Loggia	14 Master Bathroom	23 Laundry
6 Bathroom	15 Den	24 Office
7 Dining Room	16 Bedroom Suite	25 Gallery Hall
8 Butler's Pantry	17 Garage	26 Casita
9 Powder Room	18 Wine Cellar	

7,171 SQUARE FEET

About The Floor Plan: Influenced by rural Mediterranean antecedants, the plan is defined by groups of simple, rectilinear shapes. Oriented toward the sea, the house opens at the entry foyer to a finely crafted central courtyard, offering an unexpected view of the whole house. With livability focused on the main floor, the home is enhanced with a two-story casita at the entry, an artist loft and office on the upper floor, and a fitness room, wine cellar and home theater below.

Opposite Page | Hand-applied plaster finishes, exposed rafter tails and flourishes of wrought iron reference elements of rural Italian villas at the courtyard. An open foyer overlooks the central courtyard, which functions as an outdoor living area, linked to a wine cellar and wine tasting room via French doors.

Opposite Page Above | An intimately scaled foyer intersects the plan at the entry, creating a spatial connection between the forecourt and the central courtyard, and linking the formal and private wings of the home.

Opposite Page Below | A fusion of coastal influences creates a striking balance of clean, cosmopolitan lines and rural character in the formal dining room. The muted palette of sand-pebble hues provides an ideal canvas for the space's more striking furnishings.

Above | Rough stone walls and a timber ceiling alter the depth and dimension of the informal living area viewed from the open kitchen. A scalloped, square arch adds subtle definition to the space, accentuated by a shift to hardwood from travertine floors.

Above | Open to views of the ocean, the master bedroom offers a seamless boundary to the rear terrace, pool and deck. The deep, umber tones of the hardwood floor are contradicted by the sleek lines of a marble fireplace surround.

Below Left | The vintage garden tub sets the tone in the master bath, which offers splendid amenities, such as a walk-through closet, separate lavs and vanities, and a step-in dual shower.

Above | Sliding French doors open the upper-level artist's loft to the upper loggia, where wide views of the horizon are absorbed by the interior. Three windows—like ship's portals—bring in natural light and long thoughts of the sea.

Below Right | Timber trusses and a flagstone deck add dimension and color to a partially enclosed sitting area at the upper loggia. Ocean breezes flow through the space even when the drapes are closed.

Opposite Page | The purity of the design stems from the symmetry that is evident at the central courtyard—a playful, unexpected element that brings light into the core of the home. Varied textures of wood, stone, timber and brick soften the scale of the home, and call up ageless traditions that add depth to its character.

Right | French doors open the house to the amenities of the back property, a fitting environment for owners who love the outdoors. A blend of natural materials—clay roof tiles and timber beams—authenticate the elevation's rural theme.

Above | Located near the top of a hillside, the waters of a lap pool appear to rise to the level of the sea. An extensive terrace provides unobstructed views for lounging sunbathers.

Below | At the edge of the rear property, a pergola shelters an outdoor eating area, adjacent to an alfresco kitchen packed with luxe amenities such as dual commercial-grade grills.

Above | At the rear elevation, a simple stone-clad central mass is flanked by single-story stucco structures, evoking the scale of early Tuscan homes. A covered staircase connects the levels of a two-story loggia that increases light and circulation throughout the plan.

Bella Fioré
at Lake Las Vegas

BUILDER: PARDEE HOMES • LOCATION: HENDERSON, NEVADA
PHOTOGRAPHY: ERIC FIGGE

THE COMMUNITY

Set against the wide-open scenery of the high desert, this community of courtyard homes overlooks the jagged outcroppings of hillsides surrounding an area well within view of the famed Las Vegas Strip. Influenced by Andalusian, Tuscan and Italian Renaissance design themes, the houses employ cultured stone and barrel tile to create harmonious links to the environment. A stone's throw from the amenities of Lake Las Vegas Resort, the neighborhood is a natural extension of the waterfront community, with a precisely orchestrated look that pairs recessed entries, forecourts and courtyards with the varied rooflines of a village environment. One- and two-story elevations engage well-scaled proportions and traditional details—bracketed cornices, classic brick arches, overhanging eaves and sculpted columns—to underscore their link to the past, yet the homes are flexible, highly functional and environmentally friendly. Walls of glass convey a pleasing sense of space inside, integrating wide panels of scenery with rooms that also provide a sense of protection and shelter.

Above | Elemental materials, varied rooflines and broken massing create a gracious, human-scaled elevation, invigorated by textured planes, deeply recessed windows and a bold tower that harbors the entry.

Opposite Page Above | Granite-slab countertops and maple cabinetry complement sleek stainless-steel appliances in a gourmet kitchen designed for two cooks. A sculpted passageway leads to the formal dining room through a well-equipped butler's pantry.

Opposite Page Center | An open arrangement of the family room, morning nook and kitchen creates interplay between the cool polished tones of the food-preparation area and the cultivated look of the rear garden.

Opposite Page Below | Views extend beyond the rear perimeter to a spacious yard that repeats the pure, linear dimensions of the house. A covered loggia unites the master wing with an informal eating area, exemplifying the home's indoor-outdoor aesthetic.

Opposite Page Above | Amenities in the spa-like master bath include a step-in dual shower, a garden tub and a well-organized walk-in closet. A leaded-glass window and a recessed vanity affirm the lush character of the owners' retreat.

Opposite Page Center | In the gourmet kitchen, paneled cabinetry and a midnight-black tiled backsplash contribute to the European feel of the home. A crescent-shaped island orients the work spaces toward the morning room and overlooks the back property.

Above | Pure-white brackets and overhanging eaves play counterpoint to a barrel-tile roof and Venetian-red plaster on an elaborate façade derived from the villas of Italy. The forecourt leads to a foyer and an inviting transition to the formal living spaces.

Opposite Page Below | Stepped massing at the rear elevation creates separation of the outside spaces, which include a quiet courtyard accessed from the living room. Transom windows accentuate the curved wall of glass that brightens the vaulted family room.

Shady Canyon Residence

LOCATION: IRVINE, CALIFORNIA • PHOTOGRAPHY: ERIC FIGGE

W ithin a master-planned community fringed by a nature preserve and surrounded by coastal wilderness, the rubble-stone elevation of this custom courtyard home captures the spirit of a rugged Tuscan farmhouse. At the front of the plan, a 1½-story presentation conveys the simplicity of a rural villa and assigns a human scale to the streetscene. An understated forecourt allows glimpses of the central courtyard from the outside, and adds depth and dimension to a processional approach to the formal entry. Anchored by a central turret, the two-story rear elevation frames the central courtyard, which activates the primary living areas, infusing the rooms with natural light. Defined by a series of open spaces, the courtyard is enhanced with pavers and small gardens, and fused by a palette of natural materials. Inside, half-walls and flagstone steps combine with stairs and arches to define the multiple levels. At the upper courtyard, the steel-and-glass doors of a home office open on a graveled path that crosses to a covered court. Four steps lead to a lower-level fountain court that visually extends the casual living areas. Rooms on the upper floor benefit from the union of light and air brought in by a Juliet balcony overlooking the outdoor arena.

About The Floor Plan: A rectangular footprint encircles a courtyard that penetrates the plan on two levels, unified by a textured elevation of brick, stone and stucco. Single-level wings to the front of the plan provide both public and private spaces: a home office, guest quarters and a game room. To the rear of the plan, first-floor rooms radiate from a rotunda and stairwell, and lead to an open arrangement in the informal zone.

Second Floor

Opposite Page Above | Two distinct ceiling treatments permit a varied approach to the design scheme. In the family room, umber-hued beams offer contrast to the crème-colored ceiling.

Opposite Page Below | The linear proportions of the kitchen and morning nook are offset by rugged timbers and a plank ceiling above a wall of golden fieldstone. An arch of stacked brick articulates the boundary between the serving and eating areas.

Previous Page | Brick, stone, wood and iron dominate the public view of the central courtyard. Sequestered by a massive entry door, a narrow forecourt is framed by two rugged fieldstone piers and a brick arch.

Legend

1 Forecourt	8 Living Room	15 Home Office	22 Bedroom
2 Central Courtyard	9 Dining Room	16 Maid's Room	23 Master Bedroom
3 Covered Courtyard	10 Butler's Pantry	17 Laundry	24 Master Bathroom
4 Home Theater	11 Walk-in Pantry	18 Bathroom	25 Deck/Balcony
5 Game Room	12 Kitchen	19 Guest Bedroom	
6 Powder Room	13 Morning Room	20 Garage	
7 Entry Rotunda	14 Family Room	21 Loggia	

5,791 SQUARE FEET

Above | Playful lines at the entry artfully define the separation of the upper and lower floors. Corridor views extend the transitions to the living room and a gallery hall.

Right | The change in levels from the entry rotunda to the living room creates a purposeful division of space at the center of the home. An intimate grouping encircles the fireplace, which offsets the subdued spirit of the room with a commanding stone surround.

Above | Terracotta tile rooftops set among groves of cypress and olive trees bring to mind clusters of rural Italian houses perched on a scenic crest above the sea. The house is set in a community encompassing acres of canyons, hills and open spaces.

Opposite Page | A merger of house and garden occurs in the courtyard, where tile and stone create a unifying simplicity. French doors open the secluded home office to contemplative surroundings. Four steps down, an elegant stone fountain aligns with a set of glass doors leading to the family room.

Above | A covered side courtyard with an alfresco fireplace harbors an informal conversation group, adjacent to the home theater and a few steps from the game room. Heavy timber beams line the ceiling of this open-air room, designed to be simpatico with fieldstone walls and a floor of weathered-brick pavers.

Below | An olive tree casts shadows on the quiet side terrace and herb garden, where architectural forms of stone and tile step into the landscape. The through-fireplace is shared by the courtyard adjacent to the media room.

Above | Oriented toward the rear property, the upper-level master suite opens to a private deck with wide views of the preserved open spaces. Rough-hewn plank and beam ceilings contribute to the provincial charm of the owners' retreat, which provides a through-fireplace to the dual bath.

Below | Deep windows and recessed arches punctuate the two-story rear elevation. The simple rectangular massing is reminiscent of rural Mediterranean farmhouses. A covered loggia shelters an outdoor sitting area from the glare of the noonday sun.

Elements of
Design

Exterior Materials To The Inside

■ Eminently livable inside and out, this fresh interpretation of a rustic field-stone villa imparts a sense of the past to a comfortable home infused with a modern aesthetic. Tuned to the natural setting, the Tuscan-style plan introduces structural and design elements that create pleasing adjacencies with traditional materials. Rough-hewn corbels set off craggy stone piers and brick-laden arches in the courtyard, a theme that is repeated indoors with heavy timbers, ledgestone, tile and bricks. A steady play of natural materials throughout the interior erases the distinction between even the formal rooms and the outdoors. A pur-

poseful confrontation of elements occurs at boundary transitions from the courtyard to refined areas of the home: the entry rotunda, for example, exhibits a vibrant mix of renaissance themes, with thick Roman arches, terracotta pavers, sculpted wrought-iron balusters and mosaic stair tiles. Sleek metal-and-glass doors affirm the contemporary nature of the home office and media room. Every corner of the home exhibits warmth and vitality made tangible by the presence of natural exterior materials. The primal qualities of each room reconcile a needed sense of safety and shelter with the innate pleasures of living outdoors.

Tremezzo at Lake Las Vegas

BUILDER: PARDEE HOMES • LOCATION: HENDERSON, NEVADA • PHOTOGRAPHY: ERIC FIGGE

RESIDENCE TWO

Overlooking Lake Las Vegas, this Mediterranean retreat encircles a central courtyard, open to the sky and wrapped by a tile-roofed colonnade. At the front of the home, a strong, weathered-brick turret harbors a vaulted portico that creates passage to the formal entrance through the forecourt. Asymmetrical rooflines establish a varied rhythm for the façade, so that the house appears to be formed by many buildings, simulating a hilltown structure. An L-shaped loggia, defined by spiral columns and wide, sculpted arches, lines the private core of the home and articulates the positive outside space. A gallery and open rooms are organized around the center court, amplifying circulation and increasing light throughout the plan. A spacious great room extends the ambience of the courtyard to the covered patio via double sets of French doors. Surrounded by fairways and within walking distance of Lake Las Vegas village, the master-down home offers a resort environment with plenty of room for friends and visitors. Interior living spaces offer site lines oriented toward wide views captured through walls of glass. The informality of the home is expressed by the order and versatility of the interior spaces: a family room or media center off the patio, a morning room adjoining the courtyard, a flexible, upper-level club room and a main-level home office that converts to a theater, den or fourth bedroom.

Legend

1 Entry Portal	7 Morning Room	13 Master Bedroom
2 Loggia	8 Laundry	14 Master Bathroom
3 Central Courtyard	9 Family Room	15 Bedroom
4 Living Room	10 Garage	16 Guest Suite
5 Dining Room	11 Gallery Hall	17 Home Theater
6 Kitchen	12 Powder Room	18 Club Room

3,726 SQUARE FEET

Second Floor

COPYRIGHT ©2007 BASSENIAN / LAGONI ARCHITECTS

About The Floor Plan: Designed as a second home for grown families and empty-nesters, the 1½-story plan combines an informal arrangement of rooms with a large, central courtyard. Seamless transitions to the outside are provided by rows of French doors, which integrate the rear patio into the home. Near the master retreat, secondary suites are granted access to the courtyard via a gallery hall. An exterior staircase leads up to a club room that offers a grand view of the pool and spa and converts to guest quarters.

Above | Spiral columns and massive arches frame the center courtyard, anchored by an outdoor fireplace and wrapped with a loggia that shelters and subdues the space between the open-air living area and the house.

Right | Fractured massing at the rear elevation reveals Mediterranean instincts with a colonnade and a ribbon of clerestory windows. A shallow underwater deck permits the pool to lap the feet of a line of chaise lounges.

Casa Bonita del Rio

LOCATION: RANCHO SANTA FE, CALIFORNIA • PHOTOGRAPHY: ERIC FIGGE

Historic Rancho Santa Fe provides a perfect backdrop to the Early California theme of this one-of-a-kind home. Like an early-day *casa de pueblo*, a subdued entry framed by a vintage, Mission-style façade conceals a highly livable retreat of high-beamed ceilings, rustic stone arches and cool tiled floors. Mission influences inspired by the original masterworks of such regional luminaries as Wallace Neff and Lilian Rice translate easily to the open-air galleries of this single-level plan. Set on ten acres, the home fully engages its surroundings with outdoor entertainment areas, including a lush pool-and-spa environment and two loggias that ease the transitions from indoors to out. Sight lines extend the width of the house in two directions from the entry rotunda along the spine of the home, and offer engaging vistas of the back property. Flourishes of desert hues and rugged textures assign an authentic character to the home—a hacienda-style ranch house with strong ties to the outdoors. Vaulted arches add a wealth of character to individual rooms without detracting from the visual harmony and fluent dimensions that unite the home with its natural setting. Rows of windows bring in broad panels of scenery throughout the home, while along the rear perimeter, sliding glass walls achieve a seamless integration with the landscape.

Above | Heavy timber beams play harmony with a series of clerestory windows designed to offer privacy and glimpses of daylight. A brick archway frames a tranquil view of the front courtyard and fountain.

Previous Page | Varied rooflines accentuate the massing of the elevation, an asymmetrical arrangement of forms anchored by a central entry turret. A carved door opens to the *portal*, or entry hall, derived from Mission dialects.

Opposite Page | High-volume planked ceilings expand the vertical dimensions of the informal zone, a flexible entertainment area linked to the back property via a wide loggia. A raised-hearth fireplace with an intricately decorated tile surround offers a visual foil to the grand scale of the space.

Rimrock Summit

BUILDER: MASTERCRAFT HOMES

LOCATION: HIDDEN MEADOWS, CALIFORNIA • PHOTOGRAPHY: LANCE GORDON

THE COMMUNITY

This resort-style hilltop neighborhood caters to upscale professionals, employing a diverse architectural scheme, tailored amenities, flexible interiors and views that stretch westward to Catalina Island. Set in hilly terrain pocketed with boulders and swaths of chaparral, houses orient toward the distant sea, with outdoor retreats that overlook olive groves and other indigenous growth. Santa Barbara and Tuscan exterior styles with a menu of floor plans and options alter the look and function of individual homes, and create a custom-home feel throughout the community. The plans feature formal entries, stair halls and large public rooms, many of which capture the fifty-mile vista. Arched windows, precast-stone columns, brick turrets and hipped roofs contribute to design authenticity. Forecourts, porticos, casitas and sheltered porches reinforce the architectural expressions. Inside, open arrangements of the living and dining rooms, with vaulted foyers and balcony overlooks, complement impressive informal areas that connect easily with the outdoors. Versatile spaces—game rooms, dens, home offices and guest quarters—are marked by open archways and easy transitions that promote the function and flow of the homes.

Below | The open arrangement of the family room and kitchen, with a subtle sense of separation provided by a square arch, creates striking interior vistas. Paneled walls reference the kitchen's cherry-colored wood cabinetry and hardwood floors, visually uniting the area.

Opposite Page Top | A trio of clerestory glass panes allows glimpses of sky above a Palladian-style window that enriches the living room with views of the horizon. A sculpted arch opens the space to the formal dining room; the through-fireplace is shared with the adjacent den.

Opposite Page Center | The upper-level master suite provides a sitting area that opens to an expansive deck through a single French door. Light and views permitted by the large panel of windows enhance the connection to the outdoors.

Opposite Page Bottom | A series of arches creates a site line from the entry to the family room. Designed as a casual gathering space and command-central for traditional events, the kitchen offers flexible dining options.

Castellina at Covenant Hills

BUILDER: CENTEX HOMES • LOCATION: LADERA RANCH, CALIFORNIA • PHOTOGRAPHY: ERIC FIGGE

TOWNHOMES & FLATS

Stacked stone, terracotta tile and ochre-colored stucco call up the rugged, earthen forms of Italy's hill country in this prominent neighborhood of flats and townhomes. Streets follow the quiet contours of slopes and banks that wind through the community and conclude in idyllic destinations: circular piazzas wrapped by cul-de-sacs that layer even the primary traffic arteries with a sense of nature. Village trails link to parks and public spaces and maintain a friendly dialogue with the landscape. Tuscan-inspired exteriors reflect a spirited style yet express an affinity for the rural themes of the Italian originals. Multifaceted forms typify the low-pitched lines and fractured massing of the Mediterranean design, redefined as a diverse network of attached villas. Hipped and gabled rooftops and asymmetrical forms create a rhythm that tempers the scale of the structures and preserves a sense of intimacy. The imposing geometry is punctuated by rows of windows that open the homes to light and views. Covered loggias, verandas and decks invite the natural environment into the public and informal zones, and function well as outdoor rooms.

Previous Page | A playful informality prevails at the rear perimeter, where a series of courtyard-like settings enliven the balance of stucco, brick and wood. Fractured massing produces natural clusters of townhomes and flats, creating patterned angles of light that activate the individual units.

Opposite Page | Recessed double-sash windows set off a balance of stucco and stone on the exterior elevations, which swing side-loading garages away from the street thus reducing the dominance of the garage doors.

About The Floor Plan: Situated on an elevated site, the community contains 82 homes on approximately 11 acres, an arrangement that takes advantage of wonderful views. Organized into scaled neighborhoods by a spine street and its tributaries, the community also uses portal-type entry roads and sloped banks encircling land masses to further define its softscape boundaries. Two different building types offer varied elevations: two-story luxury plexes with individual covered loggias and verandas; and flats and multi-story units—such as a tri-level design with a loft retreat—linked to decks and verandas.

Above Left | The central element of this single-story floor plan is the formal dining room, a space that connects to the kitchen and living room, and leads outside to the covered loggia.

Left | An upper-level secondary bedroom enjoys plenty of light brought in by tall windows and a French door leading to a Juliet balcony. The suite provides a built-in planning desk, dual wardrobe and a private entertainment bar.

Below Left | This plan's simplicity is most evident in the living room, dining area and kitchen, where a square arch frames views and defines sight lines from one room to another.

Above | A broad square arch offers subtle definition to the family room and kitchen spaces at the front of this plan, expressing an airy aesthetic that is modern and cool. Hand-troweled ceilings, paneled beams and arches and cherry-stained floors create a pleasant ambiance.

Elements of
Design

Bringing The Outdoors In

■ Spacious patio areas in this award-winning townhome village accommodate outdoor rooms that significantly extend the livability of the interiors. The sloped site permits the building clusters to exploit valley views throughout the community, with floor plans oriented toward the rear perimeter. French doors take in the scenery and activate interior spaces with links to open-air verandas, patios and decks. Layered massing and asymmetrical forms permit daylight to enter the homes at oblique angles, creating interplay between the rear edges and streams of light. Rooms are allowed to dissolve into natural settings, infusing these reflections of old-world houses with a modern sense of space. Proportioned to accommodate conversation groups and informal meals, the outdoor rooms are furnishable in size and provide an airy place allied to indoor living areas. Timber beams and wood trellises offer a warm contrast to precast columns and stone floor tiles, contributing to the defining characteristics of the style. A series of brick-lined arches marks the rear perimeter of several plans, framing the views and creating a signature look to the rear elevation.

The Province

BUILDER: STANDARD PACIFIC HOMES • LOCATION: INDIAN WELLS, CALIFORNIA • PHOTOGRAPHY: ANTHONY GOMEZ

RESIDENCE FOUR

Classic architecture sets the tone for a desert community at Indian Wells. This Italianate villa reflects Old World traditions, with a recessed paneled entry harbored by a central turret that adds verticality to the single-story elevation. Bone-white plaster set off by wood-trim shutters and window elements hints at an early Mediterranean theme that is reinforced by cupola-like accents and a simple, clay-tiled roof. Airy colonnades and scores of windows open the home to wide views of the desert set against the profile of nearby Eisenhower Mountain. The formal plan progresses from the entry vestibule to a secluded living room, or parlor, through an extensive gallery that opens to the formal dining room and wraps the courtyard perimeter. Natural light brought in by a rear loggia is enhanced by spatial and visual connections to the side courtyard, which contains an inviting deck, pool and fountain. Throughout the home, sight lines draw guests into the public rooms, and help separate the entertainment areas from the quiet owners' retreat and private guest suites.

Above | Sculpted cornices and clay-tile roofs reveal the Mediterranean influences of this courtyard design. A decorative vent provides an idiomatic accent above a recessed entry and a series of unmatched windows.

Below | The side courtyard brings a sense of serenity that extends beyond the outdoor living area to the public and informal rooms, which wrap the outside space. Elements such as traditional coping of the pool and masonry pavers create an historic ambience.

Above | The gourmet kitchen boasts an island and serving counter that invites easy meals and family gatherings. Dark-stained floors and cabinets contrast with créme-colored walls and tile backsplash.

Below | A scalloped edge on the sculpted arch offers subtle definition to the space between the family room and kitchen. Carved details set apart the open arrangements of rooms throughout the home, providing separation without interfering with views.

Above | Double French doors open an airy master retreat to a private patio and spacious back property, engaging the warm, neutral tones of the interior with great outdoor vistas. Twin windows bring in glimpses of scenery and plenty of natural light.

The Province

BUILDER: STANDARD PACIFIC HOMES • LOCATION: INDIAN WELLS, CALIFORNIA • PHOTOGRAPHY: ANTHONY GOMEZ

RESIDENCE FIVE

In an established enclave of single-level residences, the home achieves a resort-style presence, with airy, informal living spaces connected to highly functional outdoor areas. At the street, layered massing shapes an asymmetrical arrangement of the central turret framed by front- and side-facing gables. The sand-colored, weathered-brick exterior conceals an innovative plan that begins with a recessed entry and portico, leading through the side courtyard to create an inviting processional to the formal entry. A secluded casita offers an easy transition from the front property to the patio and pool area, maintaining a vital link to the outdoors. The house is designed around the courtyard and covered patio, wrapping the edges of the outside living space with rows of French doors. Inside, perpendicular galleries take advantage of their ground-level orientation to capture natural light and views of the courtyard. During daylight hours, the shade offered by the covered patio adds a highly desired convenience, allowing casual meals and conversations to be enjoyed in a sheltered environment. On balmy evenings, the open courtyard inspires a deep appreciation of the dry desert climate.

About The Floor Plan: This C-shaped plan invites outdoor living, with a portico, courtyard and covered courtyard linking the home to the desert climate that surrounds it. The forward gallery opens to a formal dining room and, through a colonnade, to the family room, kitchen and nook. Oriented toward the rear perimeter and around the side/central courtyard, French doors increase light and circulation throughout the home's interior. Flexible spaces include an optional outdoor kitchen, which may be converted to guest quarters.

Legend

1	Entry Portal	9	Kitchen	17	Exercise Room
2	Casita	10	Nook	18	Bedroom Suite
3	Side Courtyard	11	Hall	19	Garage
4	Covered Courtyard	12	Powder Room	20	Bathroom
5	Entry	13	Laundry	21	Outdoor Kitchen
6	Gallery Hall	14	Retreat	22	Outdoor Dining
7	Dining Room	15	Master Bedroom		
8	Family Room	16	Master Bathroom		

3,490 SQUARE FEET

Right | Iron brackets and overhanging eaves affirm the Spanish roots of the design. Carriage lights flank a scrolled wrought-iron gate that leads through the portico to the courtyard.

Above | Cherry-colored cabinetry enriches a gourmet kitchen featuring a food-preparation island. The family room is arranged to allow family gatherings that include the cook.

Left | The side/central courtyard provides an idyllic outdoor environment for gatherings with guests or merely sunbathing. An arcade creates an airy border for the covered patio, and offers a unifying element for the arena. A detailed brick surround enriches the French doors leading to the casita.

Above | From the tiled entry hall, a series of arches telescopes toward the formal dining room, creating an impressive site line and airy boundary for the great room.

Below | A sculpted arch carved with a scalloped edge lends a subtle sense of separation to the master bedroom and the foreground sitting area, which features its own views of the back property.

Above | An outdoor fireplace with a masonry surround anchors the covered patio, and offers warmth and ambience to a generous, open-air sitting area overlooking the courtyard.

Destino at Vellano

BUILDER: SHEA HOMES • LOCATION: CHINO HILLS, CALIFORNIA • PHOTOGRAPHY: LANCE GORDON

THE COMMUNITY

Compatible arrangements of exterior styles organized on sloping lots create a village-like environment in this carefully planned neighborhood. Varying lot sizes honor the terrain, offering unique elevations at the streetscape. Authentic European themes employ stone, brick, tile and sun-washed hues to achieve harmony with the rural setting. Central courtyards create processional approaches to the formal entries of the homes. Arcaded galleries open the interiors to views and natural light, with key rooms positioned at the rear perimeters, where walls of glass and French doors connect the homes to their surroundings. Decks and covered patios enrich each plan's relationship to the outdoors.

Above Right | A central courtyard provides a generous outdoor living area with a fireplace and spatially connects the home and casita.

Right | A main-level master bedroom overlooks its hilly surroundings, and enjoys access to a covered patio shared with the breakfast room.

Below Right | In this single-level plan, a sculpted arch provides subtle definition to an open arrangement of the great room and kitchen.

The Cortile Collection at The Bridges

BUILDER: HCC INVESTORS/LENNAR COMMUNITIES • LOCATION: RANCHO SANTA FE, CALIFORNIA • PHOTOGRAPHY: ERIC FIGGE

RESIDENCE FOUR

Inspired by earlier renaissance styles, this formal Italian villa pairs a refined two-story stucco elevation with a square-pier entry. Flanked by a single-level wing, the forward vertical structure echoes the classic architectural proportions of a gentler era. Sited in a walkable community with an array of neighboring Tuscan-style estates, the home's grand symmetry conveys a street presence that is urban yet pedestrian-friendly, with the three-car garage placed at the side to preserve the vitality of the public view. As the plan unfolds, it is designed to allow spaces to take on a more relaxed scale, creating a balance that is straight-

forward yet stately. Beyond the front of this home, a side courtyard intentionally penetrates the footprint, increasing light and air at the core of the interior. The same attention to design is manifested around the elevation: at the rear perimeter, a protected loggia acts to soften the transition between the living area and the open back property. Designed to provide a sequential experience from the entry to the rear yard, the plan interposes a high-volume public zone with vistas and sightlines that extend toward the informal wing. The fluid progression of the home from the well-defined forward rooms to the open dimensions of the rear

Above | Panels of glass and French doors orient the casual living spaces at the back of the house toward views of the property and a sense of the outdoors. The earthy palette repeats the warm tones of Italian villas, while the wrought-iron balustrade is a characteristic elaboration of the style.

living spaces follows a design pattern prescribed for California, where a year-round climate calls for view-oriented informal zones. The spacious side courtyard, loggia, balcony and deck all enhance outdoor living experiences and invite an enjoyment of nature into the home. The plan integrates an elegant yet relaxed interior environment with convertible options that add flexibility: a main-level guest suite or home office, a walk-in entertainment bar or servery, and a secluded morning room that acts as an informal gathering area. Architectural details such as open beams, warm colors and simple square arches dominate the family room and kitchen. A book loft, which wraps the library, adds a sense of volume and space to the entire front of the home—another element of formality borrowed from centuries past.

About The Floor Plan: Formal rooms flank the entry of this well-scaled traditional plan. Under the library's 20-foot ceiling, an auxiliary staircase leads to an open book loft that adds a greater sense of space and light. Anchored by a central foyer, the gallery links the dining room with the courtyard via French doors, creating a connection with the outside space. A secluded master suite complements the upper-level sleeping quarters, and opens to a private deck.

Legend

1 Entry	9 Side Courtyard	17 Loggia
2 Living Room	10 Butler's Pantry	18 Garage
3 Music Room	11 Laundry	19 Book Loft
4 Powder Room	12 Wine Storage	20 Bedroom
5 Guest Bedroom	13 Walk-in Pantry	21 Master Bedroom
6 Bathroom	14 Morning Room	22 Master Bathroom
7 Dining Room	15 Kitchen	23 Deck/Balcony
8 Gallery Hall	16 Family Room	

5,234 SQUARE FEET

Second Floor

Opposite Page | Dual French doors open to the side courtyard, linking the alfresco living area to the formal dining room and to the stair hall, which adjoins a servery and wet bar. To the left, the space leads to the library and loft via a service hall.

Above | Framed by a colonnade of arches and anchored by a massive mantel and surround, the living room affirms the formality of the front of the plan. Rustic ceiling beams and glass-paneled cabinet doors give the room a desired connection to history.

Above | Paneled cream-colored cabinetry and pale leaf-green walls reinforce the soft interior motifs of the home in a kitchen designed for family gatherings as well as traditional occasions. The food-prep area adjoins a hall and butler's pantry that links to the formal dining room.

Elements of
Design

Classic Is Timeless

■ Pre-cast trim and corner elements drawn from an authentic European vocabulary contribute to this revival of Italian Renaissance style. Rows of pedimented windows flank the entry, suggesting a formality borrowed from later interpretations of the theme. Crafted brackets and detailed eaves dominate the cornice line beneath the low-pitched hipped roof, characteristic of Mediterranean design. Tonal variations in the stucco elevation enhance subtle changes of color and texture in the intentionally uneven rows of terracotta roof tiles. Significant embellishments, such as the Juliet balcony and wrought-iron balustrade above the entry, induce a pristine past with few concessions made to the passage of time. Shutters and surrounds on rows of windows replicate period features. Natural materials bestow a vintage character on the classic symmetry of the façade, which achieves visual fusion with the prevalent, more rustic, Tuscan architecture that shapes the community. True to the classic theme of the home, formal rooms are presented at the front of the floor plan, with the public areas open to the entry—an architectural element that has endured the test of time. Light is drawn into the house at the courtyard via the gallery, which serves as an axial element upstairs as well as downstairs, allowing myriad views of the outside space. Stacked architecture at the center and to the back of the plan also permits increased circulation and flow, and a sequential unfolding of the house on both levels.

The Lakes

BUILDER: LENNAR • LOCATION: RANCHO SANTA FE, CALIFORNIA
PHOTOGRAPHY: ERIC FIGGE

THE COMMUNITY

The Spanish colonial homes of The Lakes capture the spirit of Hollywood's Golden Era of architecture. Made popular by the works of such celebrated architects as George Washington Smith, Lilian Jenette Rice and Wallace Neff, these homes exhibit smooth, simple façades and balanced proportions that borrow heavily from Early California vernacular. The elevations employ a diverse range of forms, massing and heritage details to shape this community's rich street scene. Based on centuries-old Andalusian structures, the homes feature private courtyards that create harmony between interior spaces and the natural environment. Loggias, balconies and decks unite the rooms with their surroundings and effect sunny transitions to the enclosed gardens, courtyards and patios.

Above | Framed by a parabolic arch, the forecourt provides an inviting processional to the formal entry. A row of clerestory windows, underscored by a barrel-tile roof, helps define the forward loggia.

Opposite Page Above | A large, mullion window in the formal dining room brings in picturesque views of the San Dieguito River Valley. The archway to the rear of the room leads through a butler's pantry to the prep kitchen.

Opposite Page Center | With pure geometric forms, this Spanish Colonial Revival elevation creates an elegant composite of modern and heritage elements. A casita flanks the entry portico, topped by a deck and upper-level studio.

Opposite Page Below | A full complement of shed, hipped and cross-gabled rooflines defines this rear elevation, and authenticates the spirit of the plan. French doors line the loggia, and link the great room with views of the deck and pool.

Above | A graceful arcade and loggia add dimension to this rear elevation, which is further extended by a large patio with pool and decorative fountain. The asymmetry of the gables and stepped massing create natural rhythms that relate the house to its site.

Opposite Page Above | An informal arrangement of the great room and kitchen permits impromptu gatherings and conversation between guests and family. A simple square arch defines the separation between the food-preparation area and nook.

Opposite Page Below | Secluded to the side of the plan, the office is accessed from the entry foyer through an open archway. Windows allow abundant natural light to penetrate from the covered loggia and forecourt.

Wine Country Residence

AT PASO ROBLES

BUILDER: WOODY WOODRUFF CONSTRUCTION CO. • LOCATION: PASO ROBLES, CALIFORNIA • PHOTOGRAPHY: ERIC FIGGE

Quiet integrations of line and space play against the many moods of the sky in this modernist elevation, poised on the crest of a hill overlooking the coastal mountains of central California. Expressing native elements in a varied, intricate arrangement, the house retains a simple vocabulary of materials. Rugged fieldstone walls, heavy timber beams, and clay-tiled roofs replicate the rustic details of early pueblo dwellings, while parapets and a curved wall are converted to the bold, simple forms and intense colors of a contemporary exterior. Without front, side, or rear property-line constraints, the design rests organically on the hilltop, deploying crisp lines and smooth planes of color to effect unity with its surroundings. Broken into a collection of smaller buildings, the plan captures the simplicity of its setting with a series of geometric forms—rectangles and shed roofs—connected by a single curved axis. The approach to the entry is anchored by a sculpted terracotta-colored cylinder that offers contrast with the linear forms. Massive walls interlinked with small garden courtyards create transitions via sliding glass doors—portals that allow great fingers of light to penetrate the building forms. Oriented toward the sunset, the primary rooms step into the landscape and absorb views that on clear days extend for miles.

About The Floor Plan | A complex of buildings is linked by a curved axis that unifies the structure. Although the plan is not fully revealed at the entry, the entrance court immediately establishes a sense of logic, and the central gallery continues this organization from building to building through continual reference to the courtyards.

COPYRIGHT © 2007 BASSENIAN / LAGONI ARCHITECTS

Previous Page | A stacked-fieldstone wall seems to rise from the rocky outcroppings that line the entry courtyard. House and garden are animated by brightly colored art balls—playful abstract sculptures designed to add scale and introduce whimsy at the point of arrival.

Right | Configured to capture the site's 360-degree views, the house is expressed in a series of primary forms, each building comprising one "hut" of the village-like cluster. A western orientation captures sunsets at the rear perimeter, and positions the home to overlook the owners' vineyards and a forest of oak groves.

18

11

11

Legend

1 Entry Courtyard	7 Laundry/Utility Room	13 Master Bedroom
2 Central Gallery Hall	8 Storage	14 Master Bathroom
3 Great Room	9 Mud Room	15 Bedroom
4 Courtyard	10 Pool Bathroom	16 Guest Suite
5 Kitchen	11 Garage	17 Covered Terrace
6 Powder Room	12 Library	18 Equipment Area

4,526 SQUARE FEET

Above | Receding glass doors offer a seamless integration with the outdoors between the indoor living area and the terrace. Bold forms create modern expressions that counter the warm textures of tile and wood.

Right | Concrete columns, steel beams and overhanging eaves define the boundaries of the sheltered outdoor living spaces. Multi-levels of Canterra stone allow ample spaces for open-air conversation groups, and create an engaging interplay with the rocky terrain.

Above | A triple-window view of the side property infuses the south-ern-most guest suite with a sense of nature. Wood ceiling panels conceal lighting fixtures that indirectly add a sense of warmth and vitality to the room.

Right | In the great room, views of the distant horizon mingle with elements of a modernist vocabulary. Pure shapes and sweeping lines unite the primary living space with an eloquent assemblage of light.

Above | Geometric forms pervade the primary rooms of the house, subdued by a mix of rustic and urbane materials. Raw timber beams contradict an intricate neon wall sculpture that adds splashes of sapphire, chartreuse and amethyst to the room's neutral palette.

Opposite Page | Harbored within the cylinder, the library offers a dramatic vista of the rolling hills to the east through a tall glass portal that blurs the boundary between indoors and out.

Above | Characterized by honest, unornamented materials, the master bedroom achieves integrity with its surroundings via glass portals that open to a garden courtyard.

Right | Beyond the cloud-white walls of the master bath, hilly stretches of oak groves and vineyards roll toward the coastal mountains—a view that becomes an integral part of the architecture and aesthetic of the home.

Above | The house is centered around the gallery, a curved axis which forms a passageway connecting the main living areas and organizing the flow and circulation of the home. Among the sculptures that line the hall, two wicker balls announce the entrance to the library.

Elements of
Design

Blending With The Environment

■ Like a village on the hilltop, the house responds to the site with a simple fusion of contrasting forms and minimalist details that engage the character of the rural surroundings. The individual qualities of each building are respected with organized rhythms of scenery that promote flow to the outside spaces. Spun with the basic architectural materials of steel, concrete, wood and plaster, the design conveys a sense of the outdoors through the use of stone and other natural elements on the inside. Bold forms that reach beyond the roofline are designed to create a dialogue between land and sky, and accentuate the exterior shapes. Garden spaces between the buildings are carefully located to permit daylight and glimpses of the view via glass window and door panels. Structural lines designed to obey the slope of the site create a contemporary framework for the strong colors and varied textures of wood and tile, softening the scale of the home. In a land of contrasts, the home exhibits versatility in its integrations of spatial, structural, and utility elements, and above all, its natural link to the surrounding environment.

Three-65 at Victoria Gardens

BUILDER: SHEA HOMES • LOCATION: RANCHO CUCAMONGA, CALIFORNIA • PHOTOGRAPHY: WILL HARE, JR.

An upscale collection of flats and townhomes, this neighborhood of attached residences represents a modern composite of Prairie architecture. Horizontal lines and low-pitched, hipped roofs typify the vernacular, adapted here to a compact urban scale suited to a mixed-use community. Layered surfaces and four-sided architecture create interest on the public and private sides of the buildings. Below the roof line, mullion patterns, which are inherent to Prairie and Bungalow styles, give emphasis to groupings of windows that dominate the elevations. Massive square piers that define outdoor living areas—a universal feature of this architecture—break the symmetry of the upper-level structures. Below the decks, large porches encased in red brick with arched, hearth-style openings symbolize the broad, flat chimneys of this vernacular. A third-story loft in one of four floor plans creates a tower room on one end of the building, adding asymmetrical elements to the roof planes.

Above | Interior windows lining an upper-level master suite overlook the living room. Light pours into the space through four clerestory windows, which add to the daylight brought in by a main-level picture window.

Above Right | In the kitchen, a peninsular counter doubles as a pass-through to a flexible space in the living area that has been converted to the dining room. The rectilinear pattern of the flooring echoes the horizontal bands and subtle dark-light geometry that typify the style.

Below Right | Vibrant combinations of brick, masonry and clapboard siding define the horizontal planes of the building. Wrought-iron rails and the use of brick and other materials lend a Prairie identity to the plan.

Altamura

BUILDER: WILLIAM LYON HOMES • LOCATION: LAGUNA HILLS, CALIFORNIA • PHOTOGRAPHY: ERIC FIGGE

RESIDENCE THREE

Nested high in the foothills at Nellie Gail Ranch, this clapboard-and-brick façade conceals an engaging 21st-century courtyard plan that adds light to the interior with an array of outdoor spaces. Dual porches, including one that wraps around a flexible home office or library, highlight the traditional East Coast exterior, which positions the swing garage away from the public view to create a pedestrian-friendly approach to the home. Designed to blend with the streetscape of the twenty-year-old neighborhood, this new home preserves the heritage of the region while integrating a modern, multi-function court to enhance the flexibility and flow of the plan. Inside, the entry foyer yields to a main gallery that permits access to both the covered and open areas of the central court, pro-viding an airy boundary for the dining room and stair hall. Traditional rooms are linked by the corridor, which floods the spaces with natural light from the court-yard via a series of French doors. Great views abide throughout the plan, and the home's relationship with the courtyard does more than expand the rooms. Designed to permit maximum light into the home, the perimeter edges forward and back, creating layers of spaces that transition from indoors to out. The living room employs tall windows to bring in a sense of the outdoors, and even the secluded library enjoys a connection to nature, wrapped by a spacious front porch. Upstairs, the master suite stretches across the width of the plan, provid-ing access to decks on both sides and permitting light to enter the home.

Second Floor

Legend

1 Entry Porch	10 Dining Room	19 Garage
2 Entry	11 Kitchen	20 Porch
3 Powder Room	12 Nook	21 Library/Loft
4 Living Room	13 Butler's Pantry	22 Master Bedroom
5 Home Office/Library	14 Walk-in Pantry	23 Master Bathroom
6 Gallery Hall	15 Family Room	24 Deck/Balcony
7 Side Courtyard	16 Bedroom	25 Game Room
8 Central Courtyard	17 Bathroom	
9 Covered Courtyard	18 Laundry	

5,776 SQUARE FEET

Opposite Page | Cloud-white clapboard siding sets off a central brick gable on a classic Northeastern elevation configured with broad outdoor spaces. An intimate sitting area softens the transition to the street and invites interactions with passers-by.

Previous Page | In the central courtyard, sculpted arches set in a brick wall frame a dual-sided fireplace, repeating the exterior materials of the home. A master deck overlooks the sitting area, while a covered patio behind the courtyard offers space for outdoor meals sheltered from the sun.

Foxfield

BUILDER: PARDEE HOMES • LOCATION: YORBA LINDA, CALIFORNIA • PHOTOGRAPHY: JEFF SMITH

RESIDENCE THREE

More cutting edge than convention, this courtyard home integrates a compelling mix of authentic materials with intuitive yet intellectual design. From the street, the home appears carved from the heart of Americana: a traditional exterior of classic clapboard siding—the color of fresh cream—enriched by a grey tile roof and a gable of decorative stone. Authentic details such as double-hung sashes, red-brick lintels and an upper-level balustrade reinforce the rural vocabulary, retuned to an appealing urban scale. The sheltered porch sets off a varied roofline that mimics the terraced terrain and helps to unite the plan with its hillside location. Inside, the plan offers a highly functional, 21st-century character with multiple living options and playful, unexpected spaces that heighten the versatility of the home. The side-court plan permits an exceptional degree of customization. Just off the entry, a bedroom suite converts to a home office, while the supersized family room may be split to incorporate a separate den or guest suite; upstairs, a wide loft might become Bedroom Five. An example of a well-organized home, the highly functional design offers a great sense of space, with intimate links to the outdoors. The open living and dining room arrangement grants a sweeping view of the central stairwell and loft, adding volume and dimension to the core of the home. French doors open the dining room to the side courtyard, a secluded, informal setting that supplements the large rear yard. Natural light is invited deep into the plan, permitting many opportunities for living out-of-doors.

Previous Page Above | The neat-as-a-pin traditional exterior is accentuated by white clapboard siding, decorative stone and grey roof tiles. A balcony from the upstairs family room adds detail to the front-facing gable over the garage.

Previous Page Below | A wide balcony accessible from the owners' suite overlooks a back property designed for outdoor living, while French doors and a trio of windows bring in natural light to the supersized family room. Both the strategically placed patio and spacious backyard, located conveniently off the casual zone, offer splendid areas for open-air meals and outdoor entertaining.

Above | Steps at the landing harbor a book loft brightened by a wide archway and views of the side property. Hardwood floors mingle with plush carpeting on the upper level, with the far wing designated as living and sleeping spaces for children.

Left | Contemporary colors play counterpoint to stained maple handrails and a hardwood floor in the public realm. The stairwell and loft present sweeping interior vistas above the formal dining room, enhanced by two-level volume and views to the side courtyard.

Legend

1	Entry	7	Kitchen	13	Bedroom
2	Guest Bedroom	8	Nook	14	Laundry
3	Bathroom	9	Family Room	15	Study Area
4	Living Room	10	Game Room	16	Master Bedroom
5	Dining Room	11	Garage	17	Master Bathroom
6	Side Courtyard	12	Library/Loft	18	Deck Balcony

3,608 SQUARE FEET

Second Floor

About The Floor Plan: Oriented toward a multigenerational market, the courtyard plan achieves the targeted size of nearly 4,000 square feet, set in an articulated footprint on an elevated site. Room options expand the function of both upper and lower levels, with a high bed and bath count, and alternatives that include such luxe amenities as a game room and book loft. Outdoor spaces are notched into the periphery to the side and rear of the plan, with a master deck above that overlooks the fairway.

Montanez at Covenant Hills

BUILDER: CENTEX HOMES • LOCATION: LADERA RANCH, CALIFORNIA • PHOTOGRAPHY: ANTHONY GOMEZ

RESIDENCE ONE

Set among the hills of San Juan Capistrano, this English Country elevation presents a series of prominent overlapping gables and steeply pitched rooflines, enriched by a rustic blend of brick and stucco. Varied eave lines, exposed rafter tails and recessed windows establish today's interpretation of a 19th-century Tudor-style cottage in an upscale community of eclectic styles. Versatile areas on the main floor include an airy, well-lit dining room that relates closely to the courtyard via a covered loggia. An adjoining butler's pantry, featuring an optional sink and wine cooler, leads to a dramatic space formed by an open arrangement of the morning room, kitchen and great room. A series of French doors along the rear perimeter brings in plenty of natural light and provides access to the back property, an inviting space that complements the function of the central court.

About The Floor Plan: Designed to create a processional experience from the sidewalk to the foyer, the plan unfolds in two directions. To the left, a casita offers private access for guests via the entry portal and an independent link to the central courtyard through a rear French door. Directly ahead, a traditional foyer supported by a powder room and a coat closet establishes the formality of the home and leads to a sequence of spaces activated by sunlight from the side courtyard. Upstairs, the master retreat is extended by a hall leading to a wide tech center designed for computers and homework.

Legend

1	Entry Foyer	8	Family Room	15	Study Area
2	Casita	9	Kitchen	16	Bedroom
3	Powder Room	10	Morning Room	17	Bathroom
4	Hall	11	Butler's Pantry	18	Master Bedroom
5	Covered Courtyard	12	Garage	19	Master Bathroom
6	Side Courtyard	13	Gallery Hall		
7	Dining Room	14	Laundry		

3,846 SQUARE FEET

Second Floor

Above |The formal dining room borrows light from the covered side courtyard, expanding the visual dimensions of the home without intruding on the tranquil facets of the outdoor space.

Above | A memorable kitchen results from the creation of dual islands: one designed to host informal meals and the other dedicated as a cook station. The space is intentionally scaled to foster intimate family gatherings yet boasts the capacity to serve a crowd.

Montanez at Covenant Hills

BUILDER: CENTEX HOMES • LOCATION: LADERA RANCH, CALIFORNIA • PHOTOGRAPHY: ANTHONY GOMEZ

RESIDENCE THREE

Infused with a sense of the outdoors, this courtyard home boasts wide views of the Capistrano hills and opens to a spacious courtyard at its core. Classical elements are present in the clean lines of the clapboard elevation: square columns and balustrades evoke the grace and beauty of Seaboard Colonial houses. Reflective of the geometry of seaside vernaculars, the pure forms of the entry portico capture the tranquility of a breezy waterfront cottage. From the street, a sense of informality reinforces the coastal origins of the plan. A three-car garage is set back from the street and intentionally de-emphasized, while a deep front porch offers outdoor living and friendship to its neighbors. Inside, a time-honored arrangement of the foyer and living room leads to a grand stair hall and a formal dining room with links to the courtyard. Adjacent to the casual living area, the courtyard serves multiple functions, not the least of which is to provide a splendid outdoor retreat.

Second Floor

Legend

1 Entry Porch	8 Kitchen	15 Bedroom
2 Entry	9 Nook	16 Master Bedroom
3 Living Room	10 Family Room	17 Master Bathroom
4 Guest Bedroom	11 Covered Courtyard	18 Veranda
5 Bathroom	12 Rear Courtyard	19 Laundry
6 Dining Room	13 Garage	20 Deck/Balcony
7 Powder Room	14 Media Room	

3,730 SQUARE FEET

About The Floor Plan: Rooms positioned at the front of the plan exhibit the proportions necessary to achieve an eye-pleasing balance between the public and private sectors of the home. French doors connect the morning nook to the rear courtyard, while triple-window views of the space enrich the family room. Upstairs, a cluster of flexible spaces offers a series of links to the outdoors: a convertible bonus room provides access to a balcony linked to the master suite. Bedroom Two enjoys a private deck, while the larger bedroom suites share the veranda and views of the front property.

Previous Page | A sleek metal pavilion adds dimension and definition to the rear courtyard and harbors an intimate outdoor sitting area. Sight lines extend through an informal alfresco eating area and the covered courtyard to the formal dining room.

Opposite Page | An inviting extension of the upper floor plan, the veranda inspires fidelity to outdoor living, the enjoyment of fresh air and a love of the natural environment. A welcome counterpart to the central courtyard, this space offers a place of repose for the owners and their guests.

Above | Located to the rear of the plan, the family room extends the dramatic open space of the nook and kitchen. Surrounded by windows, the casual living area creates an airy retreat for guests and family, and links to the courtyard through the nook.

Above | Natural light filters through French doors from the court-yard to the morning nook and kitchen, illuminating cloud-white cabinetry and sleek 21st-century appliances, and amplifying the circulation of the private realm.

Front Street

BUILDER: STANDARD PACIFIC HOMES • LOCATION: LADERA RANCH, CALIFORNIA • PHOTOGRAPHY: LANCE GORDON

RESIDENCE TWO

One of California's most innovative neighborhoods, Front Street represents a practical alternative to suburban living, with a singular collection of live/work designs. A quadrant of 22 houses, the community is zoned for both commercial and residential use and presents a broad vocabulary of exterior styles that include Charleston-inspired Colonials, Monterey Haciendas and Nantucket Cape Cods. Wound with a network of pedestrian trails and paseos, the community effectively promotes a flourish of private businesses in an environment that also encourages bicycling, hiking and walking. Each plan accommodates a service-based commercial enterprise, with the placement of the work-at-home area to the front or rear, depending on the type of business. Professionals that require public interaction, such as an attorney or interior designer, benefit from a formal, street-facing entry; trades that focus on delivery-based services utilize the private loops and alleys that feed the alternate "front" doors. With the public's propensity to work at home, the project provides a ground-breaking view of live-work design, paving the way for the next great step in suburban evolution.

Elements of
Design

A Live/Work Concept

Above | Pre-wired for intelligent technology, the office space at the mezzanine (photo left) works as hard as the commercial area below (photo right). Upper-level views offer a corner-office ambience that enhances the private work area of the home.

Previous Page | A seamless approach to the outdoors is evident at the center of the plan, where a single French door expands the family's living space to a side courtyard. The loggia shelters the alfresco dining area from the sun, and leads into the work studio through a private side door.

Opposite Page Right | The rear alley entrance to the work space—the other "front door"—is as ordered and elegant as the formal streetside entrance to the home.

■ The aim: to create a house plus an office not a house that merely includes an office. The outcome: a home that delivers all of the desirable living spaces plus a private office with an effective commercial space that fits perfectly into its suburban surroundings. In refining and formalizing a practical and stylish live/work unit, necessary design distinctions emerged both in the plan forms and in the floor plan. Clearly distinguishing the residential entry to the home from the business entrance — while preserving a unified architectural character — dictated a seamless approach to the interior and outside living spaces. Creating a multi-level office space with a private-lane entrance to the rear of the plan segregates the business function and carries the Charleston-inspired, Plantation-style architecture around the home. Scaled columns, shuttered windows and clapboard siding evoke a 20th-century seaside manor, providing definition to the rear entrance. The design

3,213 SQUARE FEET

Second Floor

offers approximately 3,213 square feet, with nearly 700 square feet dedicated to the work area. Formal rooms placed to the front of the plan lead to an open arrangement of the family room and kitchen at the center, providing a transition to the work zone. Living areas are deftly connected to the whole house, with the work space/studio readily accessible from the residential zone yet not visible. Sightlines are broken by an L-shaped vestibule that subtly links to the business zone, ensuring a vital, intuitive separation of the office and family functions.

MiraBay

BUILDER: SABAL HOMES OF FLORIDA • LOCATION: APOLLO BEACH, FLORIDA • PHOTOGRAPHY: ROB/HARRIS PRODUCTIONS

TRADEWIND RESIDENCE

Tucked along the shores of an inlet of Tampa Bay, this Boca Grande home offers an excellent example of Old Florida architecture, capturing views of the water with an authentic coastal character. Horizontal wood siding, box-bay windows and a seamed metal roof are deftly crafted to showcase the authentic features of the home, a classic cross-gabled plan that strikes a balance between past and present. Highly visible from the waterside as well as the street, the elevation conveys the simple massing of the original style enlivened by an intricate notching of outdoor spaces into the front and rear of the footprint. A forecourt creates an inviting approach to a properly subdued entry; the opposing garages are turned in, away from the streetscene, to preserve the aesthetic of the public view. Along the rear perimeter, inside and outside living areas are oriented toward the waterfront—a screened lanai expands the dimensions of the core of the home and complements a starlight deck that opens the upper level to fresh air and views. The central volume contains the public spaces required for living and entertaining, framed by private sectors that lead outdoors. The master-down plan offers several convertible areas—such as the den and loft—as well as a series of playful elements, including a sunlit game room and a mid-level landing that eases the transition between the upper and lower floors.

Legend

1 Entry Porch	9 Family Room	17 Pool Bathroom
2 Entry	10 Walk-in Pantry	18 Gallery Hall
3 Living Room	11 Laundry	19 Bedroom
4 Dining Room	12 Master Bedroom	20 Bathroom
5 Lanai	13 Retreat	21 Game Room
6 Home Office	14 Master Bathroom	22 Deck/Balcony
7 Kitchen	15 Study	
8 Nook	16 Garage	

4,015 SQUARE FEET

About The Floor Plan: The straightforward H-shaped plan allows each area to open visually to the site yet permits privacy. From the foyer, a through-vista encompasses the central living and dining area, lanai and inlet. The informality of the plan is expressed by the open arrangement of rooms. Opposite the family room and kitchen, the master wing runs the full depth of the house and leads to the secondary garage, offering privacy for the owners. Upstairs, a wide loft overlooks the core living area and leads to a game room with access to the deck.

Above | A deeply set front porch runs the width of the elevation and establishes the informal tone of the house. Cloud-white Adirondack chairs inspire a sense of well-being in a setting of trim balustrades and robin's-egg-blue clapboard, wrested from the past.

Second Floor

COPYRIGHT ©2007 BASSENIAN | LAGONI ARCHITECTS

Above | Views of the bay and inlet invite repose in the owners' suite, which offers a private door to the pool and lanai. Just beyond the sleeping area, a sitting retreat defines the space with an intimate scale of its own.

Right | Oriented toward rear views, the private living and dining areas are infused with an inviting sense of informality that reinforces the seaboard character of the home. An open arrangement of the island kitchen, morning nook and family room allows for interaction between the work space and casual eating area, with plenty of places for people to gather.

Sutter's Mill

BUILDER: CENTEX HOMES • LOCATION: LADERA RANCH, CALIFORNIA • PHOTOGRAPHY: ERIC FIGGE

TOWNHOMES

Bold tones and cutting-edge lines create an award-winning tour de force in this urban-edge, high-density townhome community. Harbored by the hills of Terramor Village, Sutter's Mill reinforces the overall character of the surrounding area—a green-oriented neighborhood laced with foot trails and walkways—and connects with a network of arroyos, public courtyards and paseos that define the boundaries of the community. Fresh colors enliven elevations influenced by Bay Area row houses, Napa Valley farm buildings and historic mining structures from the Gold Rush era—revived here with striking dimensions and varied composi-

tions. Metal overhangs, cantilevered retreats and high-pitched rooflines integrate the contemporary character of the homes with the angled terrain. Carved into the setting with eco-friendly dimensions, each of the multi-plex clusters offers a quartet of distinctive plans, including a tri-level loft design. The structural purity and sustainability of each unit foster a heightened allegiance to the natural environment, a direction that has been well received by first-time buyers. A vital outcome of this approach was the community's immediate appeal to the intended market of professional singles, young couples and beginning families.

Above | An array of building forms reveals connectivity between the structures and their surroundings. The richly varied combination of textures and materials articulates the diversity of organic architecture.

Right | Colorful, upper-level retreats project above main-floor entries that address the sidewalk and connect each unit to the public realm.

Right | The turret harbors a loft retreat designed for the owners' repose. Layered massing and varied rooflines break up the scale and architectural components of the multi-plex clusters.

Opposite Page: A new concept in attached design, this high-density community features clusters of two- and three-level townhomes with pedestrian-friendly approaches and rear-loaded, direct-connect garages accessible via internal alleyways. Steeply angled rooflines and layered building forms create an informal aesthetic that is enriched with fresh combinations of lively colors. Materials such as steel-hung metal awnings and corrugated siding contrast with pure forms of wood and metal, and twist tradition toward an agrarian variation.

Elements of
Design

Fresh Colors & Eco-Sensitive Materials

■ A showcase of four-sided architecture, Sutter's Mill conveys a strong aesthetic by embracing the concept of livable, human-scaled design. Recognized with a national Best in American Living Award, a Gold Nugget for Best Attached Project, and numerous regional honors, the community is also known as a model for sustainable design. Within a green-oriented village, the homes provide a high level of energy-efficiency and sound ecological principles. Multi-layered elevations in vivid yet weathered tones mix stucco, wood and steel in innovative forms, obliques and perpendiculars, with strong lines that tower above surrounding rooftops. Branded "abstract national," the vernacular draws influence from iconic elements of farming and mining structures. Typical agrarian features, such as square turrets, balconies and steeply pitched gables, are reinvented by twisting traditional lines into a contemporized context. Corrugated siding and clapboard—time-honored vestiges of rural vocabularies—are juxtaposed against high-profile gables and projecting forms, capturing an inventive character that recalls early California dialects. Combining vibrant architecture with a reverence for nature, the townhome community merges bold, contemporary design with eco-sensitive materials. Low-VOC paints and coatings, along with water-based finishes, integrate the splashy palette of hues with a dedication to environmentalism. Steel awnings, exposed beams and commercial cabling serve as counterpoints to raised-panel entry doors—a mere hint of the hand-troweled textures and crafted works inside. The unique mix of massing and materials distinguishes these townhouses from others in the master plan, creating a visually rich, ecologically responsible community.

CHAPTER TWO

ON THE BOARDS

Umm Al Quwain
Marina & Golf Resort

BUILDER: **EMAAR** • LOCATION: **UNITED ARAB EMIRATES**
WATERCOLOR RENDERINGS: **MICHAEL ABBOTT**

Scheduled for completion in 2011, this mixed-use development plan for a 1,500-acre site along the Arabian Gulf consists of a destination-resort marina town center, upscale golf course communities, a diverse mix of retail and entertainment facilities, and exclusive recreation areas. With an extensive marina at its core, the plan unfolds with clusters of villas and townhouses on manmade islands linked by navigable waterways. This self-sustaining development partners boutique hotels, waterfront resorts, shops, restaurants and commercial buildings with open beaches, piazzas, parks and hiking trails. The environment embodies a blend of historic and modernist vocabularies. Regular rhythms of surfaces, smooth and textured, paired with atriums and courtyards that emphasize circulation and privacy, counter classical elements with contemporary themes. A primary focus on scale and the careful placement of mixed-use buildings protects the live/work ethos, while natural materials, such as stucco and terracotta, create organic links with the setting.

Al Khobar Lakes Retail Center

BUILDER: EMAAR • LOCATION: SAUDI ARABIA

The Al Khobar Lakes Retail Center is part of a master-planned community located in Saudi Arabia near the Arabian Gulf. The Retail Center is strategically positioned adjacent to the intersection of two expressways, creating a community identity while at the same time establishing a destination point for the entire development. The intent of this localized amenity is to become the focal point for social, recreational, and leisure activities for the surrounding region. Visible from a great distance, the Al Khobar Retail Center has been integrated into the regional surroundings by providing a state-of-the-art facility complementing the local architectural character. The center is positioned to respond to the various climactic conditions of the region by supplying shaded areas, natural light to the interior, and operable fenestration for cross-ventilation. Acting as a terminus, the center evokes a strong sense of procession through dramatic entry features, hierarchical spaces, and rich interior textures and materials. The center will create a destination point for day-to-day activities, such as retail shopping, dining, health and day care, as well as areas for contemplation and retreat. The intent of the facility is to establish a location for neighborhood and local interaction and exchange.

NORTH ELEVATION

Mohali Hills

BUILDER: EMAAR/MGF • LOCATION: CHANDIGARH, INDIA
GRAPHICS: AMP 3D ZONE

Designed for upscale sectors of Chandigarh, a city defined a half-century earlier by LeCorbusier, this neighborhood of homes infuses India's roots with a current aesthetic. Scaled to a landmass of nearly 1,000 acres, clusters of villas and townhomes advance the area's residential ambience to a contemporary model of planned urbanism. Rigid geometry and palettes of neutral colors convey an aesthetic expressed by cubic forms and linear dimensions, with an emphasis on proportion, scale and detail. Single- and multi-family homes, interposed on compact lots, exhibit exteriors with smooth plaster-finished walls, pre-cast concrete coping and decorative parapet caps. Entries to individual homes are designed for maximum impact. Central and side courtyards offer outside living areas, while varied levels of rooftop terraces extend private retreats. Many homes, drawn to accommodate extended families, include thoughtfully positioned stairwells, which permit a conversion to separate living quarters at a future time.

20 50 100 200
0m

MOHALI HILLS
INSPIRED LIVING

Tinja

BUILDER: EMAAR/MOROCCO • LOCATION: TANGIER, MOROCCO • RENDERING: AMP 3D ZONE

T O W N H O M E S

The architectural vernacular of the Tinja townhomes reflect a contemporary flavor with some influences from traditional motifs. The building cluster is a mixture of four attached homes — each celebrating outdoor living with courtyards, patios, balconies and roof terraces. Each home is designed with layered massing and composed to take full advantage of the nearby ocean and forest. The Tinja master-planned community is located in Tangier, an historic city in the north of Morocco that sits at the western tip of the Strait of Gibraltar where the Mediterranean Sea meets the Atlantic Ocean. This exceptional community fronts on the Atlantic Ocean on the west, a long stretch of native forest to the south and an ecologically rich river estuary to the north. At completion, the 730-acre (295-hectare) Tinja community will offer residents a vibrant town center with hotels, restaurants, a school, a beach club house, a sports facility and parks and lakes. Multiple residential offerings will include luxury villas, apartments (for-sale flats) and townhomes.

ARTIST'S CONCEPT ONLY — FINAL PROJECT MAY DIFFER

Luxury Villas
East OCT

BUILDER: OVERSEAS CHINA TOWN CO., LTD. • LOCATION: SHENZHEN, CHINA
GRAPHICS: ARCHIWOOD DESIGN DEVELOPMENT

A short drive from Shenzhen—China's center of foreign investment and one of the fastest growing cities in the world—this corporate retreat will offer repose for business executives in a secluded mountainside setting. Amid a landscape dotted with farms and lakes, the resort-style villa employs North American lodge architecture to deepen the rural character of a contemporary elevation that links closely with the outdoors. Hipped rooflines and overhanging eaves reinforce the clean simplicity of the façade's wide, horizontal layers, evoking elements of Prairie design. Decorative casement windows and sets of double French doors establish lines of symmetry supported by fieldstone and masonry piers. The plan comprises a network of rooms on four levels, which fully engage the site as the house progresses from one level to the next. Octagonal stairwells venture beyond the footprint, creating exterior paths between floors. The design reveals itself gradually, with elements of discovery planned for each space: a formal entry opens to a gallery that leads past a trio of formal spaces—a vaulted living room framed by a library and meeting room—toward a circular terminus and vectored wing that harbors the common areas, including a rustic dining hall.

Urban Infill Community

LOCATION: CALIFORNIA • RENDERING: MILO OLEA

M I X E D - U S E

A mixed-use development, this plaza provides a retail center at ground level and spacious residential flats throughout the upper floors. With a unique corner identity, the contemporary structure energizes the street with a lively palette of colors and sculpted forms. The forward-thinking residences include such features as two master suites and private balconies.

Annotated Projects List

Altamura
Residence Three
Laguna Hills, California
2003
Pages 106-109

Bassenian/Lagoni Architects Team:
Designers: Dave Pockett,
  Mike Pilarski
Project Managers: Sophia Braverman,
  John Oravetz

Builder: William Lyon Homes
Builder Executive in Charge of Design:
  Tom Mitchell
Landscape Architect: Urban Arena
Interior Designer: Design Tec Interiors
Structural Engineer: Performance Plus
  Engineering

Photographer: Eric Figge

Awards:
Best in American Living Awards 2004
  Home of the Year
National Sales & Marketing Awards 2004
  Silver Award
Gold Nuggets 2004
  Grand Award
MAME Awards/Southern California 2003
  Finalist

Bella Fioré at Lake Las Vegas
The Community
Henderson, Nevada
2006
Pages 26-31

Bassenian/Lagoni Architects Team:
Designers: Hans Anderle, Jeff Lake AIA
Project Manager: Luis Chavez

Builder: Pardee Homes
Builder Executives in Charge of Design:
  Bob Clauser, Loren Smets
Landscape Architect: SJA
Interior Designer: Color Design Art
Structural Engineer: Borm Associates

Photographer: Eric Figge

Awards:
Gold Nuggets 2006
  Merit Award
National Sales & Marketing Awards 2006
  Silver Award

Casa Bonita del Rio
Rancho Santa Fe, California
2006
Pages 48-51

Bassenian/Lagoni Architects Team:
Designers: Kevin Karami, Joe Abrajano
Project Manager: Mike Pilarski

Client: Lance and Anna Waite
Landscape Architect: Gillespie Moody
  Patterson
Interior Designer: Design Visions
Structural Engineer: Performance Plus

Photographer: Eric Figge

Awards:
Gold Nuggets 2007
  Merit Award

Castellina at Covenant Hills
Ladera Ranch, California
2005
Pages 56-63

Bassenian/Lagoni Architects Team:
Designers: Dave Kosco AIA,
  Kevin Karami, Joe Abrajano,
  Raffi Agaian
Project Managers: Jeff Ganyo,
  Ian Sparks

Builder: Centex Homes – Southern
  California Coastal Division
Builder Executives in Charge of Design:
  Richard Douglass, Nick Lehnert
Landscape Architect: Borthwick Guy
  Bettenhausen
Interior Designer: Design Tec Interiors
Structural Engineer: Van Dorpe Chou
  Associates

Photographer: Eric Figge

Awards:
Best in American Living Awards 2005
  Residence 4 – Silver Award
National Sales & Marketing Awards 2005
  Residence 4 – Silver Award
Gold Nuggets 2005
  Attached Project – Merit Award
Gold Nuggets 2006
  Community Site Plan – Merit Award
  Attached Neighborhood – Merit Award
  Community of the Year – Merit Award
MAME Awards/Southern California 2004
  Attached Community of the Year
    Winner

**The Cortile Collection
at The Bridges**
Residence Four
Rancho Santa Fe, California
2004
Pages 76-83

Bassenian/Lagoni Architects Team:
Designers: Dave Kosco AIA,
   Craig Gambill AIA
Project Manager: Brian Neves AIA

Builder: HCC Investors/Lennar
   Communities
Builder Executive in Charge of Design:
   Tom Martin
Landscape Architect: Pinnacle Design
Interior Designer: Pacific Dimensions
Structural Engineer: Performance Plus
   Engineering

Photographer: Eric Figge

Awards:
Gold Nuggets 2004
   Project of the Year – Grand Award
Gold Nuggets 2006
   Merit Award
MAME Awards/Southern California 2006
   Finalist
SAM Awards 2006 – Winner

Destino at Vellano
The Community
Chino Hills, California
2006
Pages 74-75

Bassenian/Lagoni Architects Team:
Designers: Dave Kosco AIA, Ryan White
Project Manager: Jeff Marcotte

Builder: Shea Homes
Builder Executive in Charge of Design:
   Bob Yoder
Landscape Architect: Forma Design
Interior Designer: Oma Talley Design
Structural Engineer: ESI/FME

Photographer: Lance Gordon

Awards:
Laurel Awards 2006
   Best Community – Winner
   Residence 2 – Winner
   Residences 1, 3 and 4 – Finalists

Foxfield
Residence Three
Yorba Linda, California
2005
Pages 110-113

Bassenian/Lagoni Architects Team:
Designers: John Bigot AIA, Jeff Lake AIA
Project Manager: Ian Sparks

Builder: Pardee Homes
Builder Executive in Charge of Design:
   Bob Clauser
Landscape Architect: SJA
Interior Designer: Color Design Art
Structural Engineer: Gouvis Engineering

Photographer: Jeff Smith

Awards:
ELAN Awards 2005
   Detached Community of the Year
   Finalist

Front Street
Residence Two
Ladera Ranch, California
2003
Pages 124-127

Bassenian/Lagoni Architects Team:
Designers: Dave Kosco AIA,
   Craig Gambill AIA
Project Manager: Ken Niemerski AIA

Builder: Standard Pacific Homes
Builder Executives in Charge of Design:
   Todd Palmaer, Ralph Spargo
Landscape Architect: Summers/Murphy
   & Partners
Interior Designer: Design Tec Interiors
Structural Engineer: Structural Design
   Group

Photographer: Lance Gordon

Awards:
Best in American Living Awards 2003
   Best Community – Platinum Award
   Residence 2 – Gold Award
National Sales & Marketing Awards 2003
   Residence 2 – Silver & Regional Awards
Gold Nuggets 2003
   Site Plan – Grand Award
   Residence 2 – Grand Award
MAME Awards/Southern California 2003
   Winner

Magazine Cover: Builder Magazine,
   September 2003

The Lakes
The Community
Rancho Santa Fe, California
2007
Pages 84-89

Bassenian/Lagoni Architects Team
Claybourne Product
  Designers: Kevin Karami, Joe Abrajano
  Project Managers: Jeff Ganyo,
    Brian Neves AIA, Sophia Braverman,
    Derek Sabor
Edgewater Product
  Designers: Craig Gambill AIA,
    Raffi Agaian, Ryan Sullivan
  Project Manager: Marty Lopez

Builder: Lennar
Builder Executives in Charge of Design:
  Mike Levesque, Tom Martin
Landscape Architect: Pinnacle Design
Interior Designer: Pacific Dimensions
Structural Engineer: Swanson &
  Associates

Photographer: Eric Figge

Awards:
Sam Awards 2007 – Winner
  Claybourne Product - Residence 2

MiraBay
Tradewind Residence
Apollo Beach, Florida
2005
Pages 128-131

Bassenian/Lagoni Architects Team:
Designers: Hans Anderle, Jason Yaw
Project Manager: Mike Beam

Builder: Sabal Homes of Florida
Builder Executive in Charge of Design:
  Bill Lee
Landscape Architect: Dunlap &
  Associates
Interior Designer: Creative Design
  Consultants
Structural Engineer: Silcox, Kidwell &
  Associates

Photographer: Rob/Harris Productions

Awards:
National Sales & Marketing Awards 2005
  Gold & Regional Winner
Aurora Awards 2005
  Best Detached Single Family Home
  Best Kitchen
  Best Interior Detailing
  Best Master Bath
Tampa Bay Parade of Homes 2006
  Grand Award
Tampa Bay Parade of Homes 2007
  Grand Award
MiraBay Newland Communities 2006
  Outstanding Architecture
    Grand Award

Magazine Cover: Professional Builder,
  May 2005

Montanez at Covenant Hills
Residence One
Ladera Ranch, California
2005
Pages 114-117

Bassenian/Lagoni Architects Team:
Designers: Dave Kosco AIA,
  Kevin Karami, Joe Abrajano,
  Raffi Agaian
Project Managers: Jeff Ganyo,
  Sophia Braverman

Builder: Centex Homes – Southern
  California Coastal Division
Builder Executives in Charge of Design:
  Richard Douglass, Nick Lehnert,
  Rick Wood
Landscape Architect: Borthwick Guy
  Bettenhausen
Interior Designer: Studio Design Group
Structural Engineer: Van Dorpe Chou
  Associates

Photographer: Anthony Gomez

Awards:
MAME Awards/Southern California 2005
  Best Detached Community – Finalist
    Residence 1 – Winner

Montanez at Covenant Hills
Residence Three
Ladera Ranch, California
2005
Pages 118-123

Bassenian/Lagoni Architects Team:
Designers: Dave Kosco AIA,
  Kevin Karami, Joe Abrajano,
  Raffi Agaian
Project Managers: Jeff Ganyo,
  Sophia Braverman

Builder: Centex Homes – Southern
  California Coastal Division
Builder Executives in Charge of Design:
  Richard Douglass, Nick Lehnert,
  Rick Wood
Landscape Architect: Borthwick Guy
  Bettenhausen
Interior Designer: Studio Design Group
Structural Engineer: Van Dorpe Chou
  Associates

Photographer: Anthony Gomez

Awards:
Gold Nugget Awards 2006
  Merit Award
MAME Awards/Southern California 2005
  Best Detached Community – Finalist

The Province
Residence Four
Indian Wells, California
2007
Pages 64-67

Bassenian/Lagoni Architects Team:
Designers: Kevin Karami, Raffi Agaian,
   Alan Nguyen
Project Manager: Sophia Braverman

Builder: Standard Pacific Homes
Builder Executives in Charge of Design:
   Ram Fullen, Gary Carlson
Landscape Architect: HRP Studio
Interior Designer: Meridian Interiors
Structural Engineer: Structures Design
   Group

Photographer: Anthony Gomez

Awards:
Gold Nuggets 2007
   Grand Award

The Province
Residence Five
Indian Wells, California
2007
Pages 68-73

Bassenian/Lagoni Architects Team:
Designers: Kevin Karami, Raffi Agaian,
   Alan Nguyen
Project Manager: Sophia Braverman

Builder: Standard Pacific Homes
Builder Executives in Charge of Design:
   Ram Fullen, Gary Carlson
Landscape Architect: HRP Studio
Interior Designer: Meridian Interiors
Structural Engineer: Structures Design
   Group

Photographer: Anthony Gomez

Awards:
Gold Nuggets 2007
   Merit Award

Rimrock Summit
The Community
Hidden Meadows, California
2006/2007
Pages 52-55

Bassenian/Lagoni Architects Team:
Designers: Ray Hart, Stacie Arrigo
Project Managers: Jeff Ganyo,
   Mike Beam, Marty Lopez

Builder: Mastercraft Homes
Builder Executives in Charge of Design:
   Daniel Thompson, Bob Liewer
Landscape Architect: Land Concern
Interior Designer: Blackbird Interiors
Structural Engineer: Gouvis Engineering

Photographer: Lance Gordon

Awards:
Gold Nuggets 2007
   Detached Community – Merit Award
   Residence 1 – Merit Award

Shady Canyon Residence
Irvine, California
2006
Pages 32-43

Bassenian/Lagoni Architects Team:
Designers: Kevin Karami, Joe Abrajano
Project Manager: Jeff Marcotte

Client: Jeff Roos
Landscape Architect: Katzmaier Newell
   Kehr
Interior Designers: Dana Blower Design,
   Christopher Kinne
Structural Engineer: Gouvis Engineering

Photographer: Eric Figge

Sutter's Mill
Ladera Ranch, California
2004
Pages 132-137

Bassenian/Lagoni Architects Team:
Designers: Dave Kosco AIA,
Steven Dewan AIA, John Bigot AIA
Project Managers: Jeff Ganyo,
Ian Sparks

Builder: Centex Homes – Southern
California Coastal Division
Builder Executives in Charge of Design:
Richard Douglass, Nick Lehnert
Landscape Architect: Borthwick Guy
Bettenhausen
Interior Designer: Rooms Interiors
Structural Engineer: Van Dorpe Chou
Associates

Photographer: Eric Figge

Awards:
Best in American Living Awards 2004
Best Attached Project – Platinum Award
National Sales & Marketing Awards 2004
Residence 4 – Gold and Regional Awards
Gold Nugget Awards 2005
Attached Project – Grand Award
Attached Project of the Year –
Merit Award
Gold Nugget Awards 2004
Best Attached Project – Merit Award
American Institute of Architects/Orange
County 2004
Honor Winner
MAME/Southern California 2004
Attached Project – Finalist

Magazine Cover:
Professional Builder, November 2004

Three-65 at Victoria Gardens
Rancho Cucamonga, California
2007
Pages 104-105

Bassenian/Lagoni Architects Team:
Designers: Dave Kosco AIA, Raffi Agaian
Project Manager: Scott Bunney

Builder: Shea Homes
Builder Executive in Charge of Design:
Bob Yoder
Landscape Architect: The Collaborative
West
Interior Designer: Garrett Interiors
Structural Engineer: ESI/FME

Photographer: Will Hare, Jr.

Awards:
Gold Nugget Awards 2007
Attached Project – Merit Award
Attached Project of the Year –
Merit Award
Builders Choice 2007
Grand Award Winner
Best in American Living Awards 2007
Best Single Family Attached –
Platinum Award

The Tides at Crystal Cove
Residence One
Newport Coast, California
2007
Pages 14-25

Bassenian/Lagoni Architects Team:
Designers: Kevin Karami,
Dave Kosco AIA, Joe Abrajano,
Project Manager: Brian Neves AIA

Builder: Standard Pacific Homes –
Gallery Communities
Builder Executives in Charge of Design:
Todd Palmaer, Ralph Spargo
Landscape Architect: Summers/Murphy
& Partners
Interior Designer: Pacific Dimensions
Structural Engineer: Structures Design
Group

Photographer: Anthony Gomez

Awards:
National Sales & Marketing Awards 2007
Residence 1 – Silver Award

Tremezzo at Lake Las Vegas
Residence Two
Henderson, Nevada
2007
Pages 44-47

Bassenian/Lagoni Architects Team:
Designers: Hans Anderle, Jeff Lake AIA,
Stacie Arrigo, Will Francisco
Project Manager: Brian Cameron

Builder: Pardee Homes
Builder Executives in Charge of Design:
Bob Clauser, Loren Smets
Landscape Architect: SJA
Interior Designer: Color Design Art
Structural Engineer: Borm Associates

Photographer: Eric Figge

Awards:
National Sales & Marketing Awards 2007
Residence 2 – Silver Award

Wine Country Residence
Paso Robles, California
2006
Pages 90-103

Bassenian/Lagoni Architects Team:
Designers: Steven Dewan AIA,
John Bigot AIA
Project Manager: Mike Beam

Builder: Woody Woodruff Construction
Company
Landscape Architect: Land Concern
Interior Designer: Marilyn Riding Design
Construction Documents: Randall Barnett
Structural Engineer: Jeffrey Schneidereit
Architects
Lighting Consultant: Linda Ferry Lighting
Design

Photographer: Eric Figge

Awards:
Gold Nugget Awards 2007
Merit Award
MAME Awards/Southern California 2007
Best Custom Home – Winner
Best in American Living Awards 2007
Best One-of-a-Kind Custom Home
Gold and Regional Winner
National Sales & Marketing Awards 2007
Best One-of-a-Kind Home 2007
Gold and Regional Award

Al Khobar Lakes
Retail Center
Saudi Arabia
2007
Pages 142-143

Bassenian/Lagoni Architects Team:
Designer: Ali Badie AIA

Builder: Emaar
Builder Executives in Charge of Design:
Mark Amirault, Nasreldain Mahamoud

Luxury Villas
East OCT
Shenzhen, China
2007
Pages 148-149

Bassenian/Lagoni Architects Team:
Designer: Wenfei Feng

Builder: Overseas China Town Co., Ltd.
Builder Executives in Charge of Design:
Jian Dian, Judy Qiao

Graphics: Archiwood Design
Development

Mohali Hills
Villa Homes
Chandigarh, India
2007
Pages 144-145

Bassenian/Lagoni Architects Team:
Designers: Albern Yolo, Robert Orosa AIA

Builder: Emaar/MGF
Builder Executive in Charge of Design:
Scott Pottruff

Rendering: AMP 3D Zone

Tinja
Townhomes
Tangier, Morocco
2007
Pages 146-147

Bassenian/Lagoni Architects Team:
Designers: Ali Badie AIA, Romeo Ty,
Kevin Karami

Builder: Emaar/Morocco
Builder Executives in Charge of Design:
Wafaa Snibla
Turner International

Rendering: AMP 3D Zone

Umm Al Quwain
Marina & Golf Resort
United Arab Emirates
2006
Pages 140-141

Bassenian/Lagoni Architects Team:
Designer: Ali Badie AIA

Builder: Emaar
Builder Executives in Charge of Design:
Scott Pottruff, Sana Farooq

Rendering: Michael Abbott

Urban Infill Community
California
2006
Pages 150-151

Bassenian/Lagoni Architects Team:
Designers: Ali Badie AIA,
Paul Fulbright AIA

Rendering: Milo Olea

Staff List 2007

Executive Staff
Aram Bassenian
Carl Lagoni
Scott Adams
Ali Badie
Steven Dewan
Kevin Karami
Dave Kosco
Jeff LaFetra
Jeff Lake
Ken Niemerski
Lee Rogaliner

Vice Presidents
Mike Beam
Robert Chavez
Ernie Gorrill
Nick Lehnert
Brian Neves
Dave Pockett

**Vice President,
China Operations**
Yao Wang

Director of Marketing
Heather McCune

**Associate
Vice Presidents**
Hans Anderle
Craig Gambill
Jeff Ganyo
Marty Lopez
Edie Motoyama
Robert Orosa

Senior Associates
John Bigot
Sophia Braverman
Ray Hart
Jeff Marcotte

Associates
Kevin Burt
Brian Cameron
Dave Day
Judy Forrester
George Handy
Curtis Ong
Tony Vinh
Wendy Woolsey

General Staff
Joe Abrajano
Raffi Agaian
Stacie Arrigo
Edwin Balquiedra
Jesse Barrera
Rafael Bello
Karen Bestone
Bruce Bishara
Randy Brown
Scott Bunney
Dwayne Butz
Eva Caranay
Lenz Casilan
Sergio Cecena
Luis Chavez
Johnny Chung
Freddy Conrado
Sue Dewan
Jenni Dillon
Kele Dooley
Dee Drylie
Maleck Elahi
Ginger Elkins
Gerry Encarnacion
Alicia Erickson
Todd Evans
Jorge Favila
Joey Feld
Wenfei Feng
Jornell Franciliso
Will Francisco
Paul Fulbright
Casey Galyean
Mike Gilbert
Kevin Groves
Joohyun Her
Young Hong
Roberta Jeannette
Alison Jones
Joel Jose
Erik Kelenc
James Kim
Alan Knebel
John Kounlavong
Huy Le
Mark Leasor
Jason Lee
Ji Sun Lee
Phillip Lee
David McClean
Kristina McVeigh
Jose Mendez

Carlos Meneses
Laura Minott
Tom Mkhitaryan
Christina Nagel
Alan Nguyen
Ronnie Ojeda
Jacob Olid
John Oravetz
Carlos Pelayo
Margo Penick
Jeremy Phillips
Mike Pilarski
Susan Pistacchi
Rachel Pockett
Gregory Purvis
Tarane Rahmani
Yvonne Ramos
Rod Reyes
Jeff Roach
Nate Rodholm
Ryan Rosecrans
Erin Ryan
Derek Sabor
Katya Sato
Selma Saxton
Jesika Scherzinger
Anna Shakun
Andrew Silder
Jeffry Sinarjo
Debora Smith
Tracy Smith
Ian Sparks
Dawn Stanton
Michael Stone
Kevin Stracner
Ellen Sung
Janet Thomas
Romeo Ty
Chris Velasquez
Linda Velasquez
April Villa
Long Vu
Warren Walker
Jill Warren
James West-Herr
Ryan White
Eric Widmer
John Wilmert
Michael Wu
Wenling Wu
Albern Yolo
Bernard Yuen

Index